Bloom's

GUIDES

Charles Dickens's
A Tale of Two Cities

The Adventures of Huckleberry Finn
All the Pretty Horses
Animal Farm
Beloved
Brave New World
The Catcher in the Rye
The Chosen
The Crucible
Cry, the Beloved Country
Death of a Salesman
Fahrenheit 451
The Glass Menagerie
The Grapes of Wrath
Great Expectations
The Great Gatsby
Hamlet
The Handmaid's Tale
The House on Mango Street
I Know Why the Caged Bird Sings
The Iliad
Lord of the Flies
Macbeth
Maggie: A Girl of the Streets
The Member of the Wedding
The Metamorphosis
Of Mice and Men
1984
The Odyssey
One Hundred Years of Solitude
Pride and Prejudice
Ragtime
Romeo and Juliet
Slaughterhouse-Five
The Scarlet Letter
Snow Falling on Cedars
A Streetcar Named Desire
A Tale of Two Cities
The Things They Carried
To Kill a Mockingbird

Bloom's

GUIDES

Charles Dickens's
A Tale of Two Cities

Edited & with an Introduction
by Harold Bloom

CHELSEA HOUSE
P U B L I S H E R S
An imprint of Infobase Publishing

Bloom's Guides: A Tale of Two Cities

Copyright ©2007 by Infobase Publishing
Introduction ©2007 by Harold Bloom

Chelsea House
An imprint of Infobase Publishing
132 West 31st Street
New York NY 10001

Library of Congress Cataloging-in-Publication Data
Charles Dicken's A tale of two citites / Harold Bloom, (editor).
p. cm — (Bloom's guides)
Includes bibliographical references and index.
ISBN 0-7910-9293-3 (hardcover)
1. Dickens, Charles, 1812–1870. Tale of two citites. 2. France—History—Revolution, 1789–1799—Literature and the revolution. I. Bloom, Harold. II. Title: Tale of two cities. III. Series.
PR4571.C483 2006
823'.8—dc22   2006031096

Chelsea House books are available at special discounts when purchased in bulk quantities for businesses, associations, institutions, or sales promotions. Please call our Special Sales Department in New York at (212) 967-8800 or (800) 322-8755.

You can find Chelsea House on the World Wide Web at
http://www.chelseahouse.com

Contributing Editor: Mei Chin
Cover design by Takeshi Takahashi

Printed in the United States of America

Bang EJB 10 9 8 7 6 5 4 3 2 1

This book is printed on acid-free paper.

Contents

Introduction

HAROLD BLOOM

Though it is, by any standard, a remarkable performance, *A Tale of Two Cities* at first may seem distinctly *not* a novel by Charles Dickens. Where are the great grotesques, the endless digressions, above all the humor? Dark and unrelenting, the *Tale* is pure storytelling, as economical in its way as is Shakespeare's *Macbeth*. Dickens even provides us with *his* Lady Macbeth in Madame Defarge, the fiercely attractive genius of the French Revolution, as the *Tale* portrays it. Nor are Madame Defarge and her husband, the wineshop keeper Defarge, the villains of the book. For once, Dickens has no villains, or history itself is the villain. Though the story manifests an obsessive dread of revolutionary violence, it also displays a considerable loathing for the social oppression that, in part, provoked the French Revolution and the Reign of Terror. Much under the influence of Thomas Carlyle's visionary chronicle *The French Revolution*, Dickens's narrative shares in Carlyle's prophetic warning to England that economic tyranny ensues at last in the answering tyranny of the mob. Whether *A Tale of Two Cities* now can be interpreted as an admonition for the United States, as it moves through the new Millennium, is for the individual student or reader to judge.

If the *Tale* has no authentic villains, despite the colorful menace of the Defarges and their followers, it also lacks heroes and a heroine, though such a view would have disheartened Dickens, who certainly intended Lucie Manette as the heroine and Sydney Carton and Charles Darnay, the two men who love her, as heroes. Unfortunately, the three of them together are likely to interest us rather less than Madame Defarge does, because they lack her intensity of being. If we read more closely, then we will find that Carton is profoundly interesting, though neither Lucie nor her husband, Charles Darnay, is redeemed as a dramatic character by prolonged scrutiny.

Carton, despite his celebrated and sentimental prophetic thoughts that close the book, is more than the dark side of his double and successful rival, Darnay. We can surmise that Carton is the near-nihilist that Dickens senses he himself might become. Whether Carton's self-sacrifice is psychologically persuasive is disputable, but it is dramatically convincing and has become a permanent image of renunciation, as Dickens intended that it should be. Though he dies *as* Darnay, and considers himself to be dying *for* Lucie, Carton in a true sense dies so that his creator, Charles Dickens, shall continue to live.

Madame Defarge, everyone's favorite character in the novel, dies a victim of her own consuming passion for revenge. Carton's closing prophecy tells us that Defarge and his group will also die, by the agency of the guillotine they have worshipped and fed. Since Dickens had little more than Carlyle's vision of the French Revolution to sustain him, *A Tale of Two Cities* is not history and hardly asks to be taken as such. The book is a historical romance in its genre, yet it would have never achieved its perpetual popularity if it were entirely composed in that mode. John Ruskin, the great Victorian critic, rightly praised Dickens as being a master of "stage fire," and *A Tale of Two Cities* in its essence is a melodrama, very appropriate for dramatic presentation, whether in the theater or on screen. The actual leaders and contending forces of the French Revolution do not appear in the book, which so arranges matters as to make us believe that a better-informed police could have prevented the upheaval by one efficient raid on the Defarge wineshop. That would be absurd history, but the book's identification of the Revolution with the Defarges is as dramatically successful as Shakespeare's concentration upon Macbeth and Lady Macbeth, while blending everyone else in the play into a common grayness. The single image everyone remembers of *A Tale of Two Cities* is Madame Defarge's knitting. She is the malevolent, would-be Fate of the novel, and her knitting hints at the weaving of the Fates, a role occupied by the witches in *Macbeth*. It is not too much to say that Madame Defarge is not only the aesthetic glory of Dickens's *Tale*, but in a clear way is the symbol or emblem that unifies the entire book. She is the image of death itself: remorseless, both frightening and yet masochistically attractive, and finally to be conquered only by heroic love, embodied (in the Dickens manner) by the very English Miss Pross, as indomitable as Winston Churchill or as Dickens himself. The vision of renunciation and the resurrection that Dickens sought to convey in Sydney Carton is far better served by Miss Pross, who is willing to die for the Darnay family but instead lives for them, and by her triumph allows them to live.

Biographical Sketch

Charles John Huffam Dickens was born in Landport, Portsea, near Portsmouth, England, on February 7, 1812, the second of eight children of John and Elizabeth (Barrow) Dickens. The family moved to London in 1814, to Chatham in 1817, and then back to London in 1822. By 1824 increasing financial difficulties caused Dickens's father to be imprisoned briefly for debt; Dickens himself was put to work for a few months at a shoe-blacking warehouse. Memories of this painful period in his life were to influence much of his later writing, in particular the early chapters of *David Copperfield*.

After studying at the Wellington House Academy in London (1824–27), Dickens worked as a solicitor's clerk (1827–28), and then for various newspapers—first the *True Sun* (1832–34) and later as a political reporter for the *Morning Chronicle* (1834–36). In 1833 Dickens fell in love with Maria Beadnell, but her family opposed marriage. Dickens never forgot Maria, and she served as the model for Dora in *David Copperfield*.

It was also around this time that Dickens began to publish in the *Monthly Magazine* and elsewhere under the pseudonym "Boz"—pronounced with a long *o*—a derivative of a nickname he'd given to a younger brother. A collection of these pieces appeared in 1836 as *Sketches by Boz*. This was followed by the enormously popular *Posthumous Papers of the Pickwick Club* (1836–37). Like many of Dickens's later novels, *Pickwick* first appeared in a series of monthly chapbooks or "parts." Other novels were serialized in magazines before appearing in book form.

In 1836 Dickens married Catherine Hogarth; the couple would have ten children together before their difficult separation in 1858. Catherine's teenage sister, Mary Hogarth, lived with them at the beginning of the marriage but died after a few months; the loss affected Dickens permanently, and Mary would become the model for many of the pure, saintly heroines in his novels—such as Little Nell in *The Old Curiosity Shop*— who die at an early age. Later, Catherine's sister Georgina assumed some of the household duties, and she and Dickens became close friends.

Also in 1836, Dickens was tapped to serve as editor for a new periodical, ultimately entitled *Bentley's Miscellany*, and it is in *Bentley's* that *Oliver Twist* began, early in 1837. Dickens continued *Twist* and *Pickwick* simultaneously, and followed with *Nicholas Nickleby* in 1838–39. Dickens then founded his own weekly, *Master Humphrey's Clock* (1840–41), in which appeared his novels *The Old Curiosity Shop* and *Barnaby Rudge*. In 1842 he and his wife visited the United States and Canada; despite the unprecedented enthusiasm they met there, Dickens found the United States so little to his taste that his *American Notes* (1842) caused a temporary scandal. The barbs against the U.S. continued in his next serial, *Martin Chuzzlewit* (1843–44), which did not see the success of his previous work.

In 1843 Dickens published *A Christmas Carol*, the first in a series of Christmas books that included *The Chimes* (1845), *The Cricket on the Hearth* (1846), *The Battle of Life* (1846), and *The Haunted Man and the Ghost's Bargain* (1848). Early in 1846 he was for a brief time the editor of the *Daily News*, a paper of the Radical party to which he contributed "Pictures of Italy," after visiting Italy in 1844 and again in 1845. During a visit to Switzerland in 1846 Dickens wrote his novel *Dombey and Son*, which appeared monthly between 1846 and 1848. In the 1850s Dickens founded two literary periodicals with political overtones: first *Household Words* (1850) and then *All the Year Round* (1859), which he would continue to edit until his death. Much of his later work was published in these two periodicals, including *David Copperfield* (1849–50), *Bleak House* (1852–53), *Hard Times* (1854), *Little Dorrit* (1855–57), *A Tale of Two Cities* (1859), *Great Expectations* (1860–61), and *Our Mutual Friend* (1864–65).

Throughout his life, Dickens threw himself vigorously into a variety of social and political crusades, such as reform of prisons, education, workhouses, and copyright law—American publishers were notorious for pirating his work. These interests find their way into his work, which is characterized by empathy for the oppressed and a keen examination of class distinctions.

His novels and stories have been both praised and censured for their sentimentality and their depiction of "larger-than-life" characters, such as Pickwick or *David Copperfield*'s Mr. Micawber.

In the last twenty years of his life Dickens made time for what may have been his first love, the theater, taking on every conceivable duty in amateur productions for charity. He also became involved in a variety of philanthropic activities. He made his second visit to America in 1867–68, as part of an endless series of readings from his works that were lucrative and fanatically received but threatened his health.

Dickens died suddenly on June 9, 1870, leaving unfinished his last novel, *The Mystery of Edwin Drood*. *Drood* was published later that same year. Several editions of his collected letters have been published. Despite his tremendous popularity during and after his own life, it was not until the twentieth century that serious critical study of his work began to appear. Recent criticism has favored the later, more somber and complex works over the earlier ones characterized by boisterous humor and broad caricature.

The Story Behind the Story

"When I was acting," Charles Dickens writes in his preface to the first edition of *A Tale of Two Cities*, "with my children and friends, in Mr. Wilkie Collins's drama of The Frozen Deep, I first conceived the main idea of the story. A strong desire was upon me then, to embody it in my own person."

"The Frozen Deep" was the brainchild of Wilkie Collins, based on his novel of the same name. In 1855 Collins approached Dickens, his mentor, to propose a theatrical production. It was not the first such enterprise for the two men; Collins had been active in many of the charity and amateur productions that Dickens had staged at Tavistock House, the small Bloomsbury theater Dickens had purchased several years before. But both men were distracted by professional commitments, and two years passed before the production finally opened at Tavistock House. Still, it was an immediate success, with Dickens at the helm as editor, producer, director, and star. By the end of that year, egged on by popular demand, Dickens and Collins took the tiny production to the professional stage.

The plot is simple, set in the dual backdrops of London and the raging Arctic. Clara Burnham, the swooning, virginal heroine of the story, is engaged to Frank Aldersley, who is on a dangerous Arctic expedition. Aldersley is joined by Richard Wardour, who also is in love with Clara but who has been spurned. Wardour when we meet him is angry, and practically debauched; he is drinking and swearing to murder the man who has taken the heart of his beloved. At the end, however, Wardour not only does not kill his rival, but sacrifices his own life to save him. Dickens's daughter Mary played the part of Clara in the original production; Collins played Frank Aldersley, and Dickens himself assumed the mantle of Richard Wardour. Dickens played Wardour with the ferocity that his audiences had come to expect from him, and that would characterize his later dramatic readings: he roared and gnashed and made them tremble and weep.

Dickens described "The Frozen Deep" as an "old fashioned melodrama," and indeed, on reading it today, "The Frozen Deep" does seem cloying. Its characters are generally flat and include a prophetic Scottish nurse who foretells the future in brogue. But Victorian audiences raved; even the Queen was moved. More importantly, the play excited Dickens, and the role of Wardour inspired him.

Dickens had been infatuated with acting since the beginning; "I was," he once said, "an actor and speaker from a baby." (Ackroyd, 38) Even as a child, he liked to recite and entertain his family with skits. His later public readings were intense one-man productions in which he not only read his characters, but *inhabited* them. As he grew older, his interactions with the world became more theatrical; when one mode of life became tiresome, he would re-stage it. It is difficult to determine exactly when this habit of self-dramatization began, but we do know that he wove into *David Copperfield* (1849–50) passages from his unpublished autobiography. By the height of his career, the boundary between reality and the more vital reality of the imagination had become unclear. Dickens did not merely act his heroes; he became them; and of all the heroes he became, Richard Wardour was his favorite.

It is interesting that this desire to escape into heroic personas intensified with age. After all, Dickens at the height of his career was a far from ordinary man. He was the Victorian equivalent of a celebrity, and where he went, what he ate, and whom he saw were subjects that excited the public imagination. However, Dickens was also a middle-aged man grappling with middle-aged problems. His wife was portly and neurotic, and though he had everything that he had ever desired as a boy— family, fame, fortune—he was unhappy. By the close of "The Frozen Deep," Dickens had staged his own drama by leaving Catherine Dickens for a young actress, Ellen Ternan, whom he had cast to play the part of Clara Burnham's friend Lucy Crayford. He probably had never felt the contrast between

Wardour and himself more keenly. Wardour had battled Arctic ice floes and sacrificed his life. Dickens had rather unglamorously walked out on his marriage. It explains Dickens's continued longing for Wardour even after the play had concluded—that "strong desire," in his words, "to embody it in my own person." We can find in Wardour the genesis of Sidney Carton, the romantic hero of *A Tale of Two Cities.*

Critical to Carton's conception was contemporary response to Richard Wardour. Problematic heroes were rare in the literature of the time, and rarer still in literature of wide circulation. Like Wardour, Carton was a drinker and a debaucher, and Dickens had never tried a hero whose behavior so tested moral boundaries. But the Victorians loved Wardour; it seemed that they could accept a damaged man, as long as nobility could be found in him.

Sidney Carton defined a new kind of Romantic hero, a man who is not born noble but becomes so by merit alone. But the similarities between him and Dickens meant the character had to be articulated with care. There was the question of age and scandal to be considered. For Dickens, it was no longer seemly to play the besotted scallywag chasing after some young thing, as Nicholas Nickleby and David Copperfield might have done. The object of his affections, Ellen Ternan, was tender and virginal, and in his much-publicized courtship of her, Dickens risked charges of lechery. Sidney Carton's hero is an older and sadder one, inspired not only by Wardour but also by Arthur Clenham of Dickens's *Little Dorrit*—who, at the age of fifty, manages to marry a girl with the face and figure of a twelve-year-old without looking perverse. Carton embodies the hero as an aging martyr. He protects rather than woos; he feels passion, but a chaste one. He is at once the lover and the father.

Dickens denied allegations of a sexual relationship with Ternan, but he did take care of her, as well as her mother and sisters, all of them struggling actresses. As a guardian rather than a lover, Dickens was able to justify his attentions. Sidney Carton, too, is more protector than lover; ensuring the safety of his beloved Lucie Manette out of desires so platonic that he saves her husband also. Not surprisingly, the audience of 1859 who might have compared Dickens and Carton might also have seen Ellen Ternan in Lucie Manette. And this may even have been Dickens's intention. Carton adores Lucie but will never have her; are we meant to think the same of Dickens and Ternan?

But *A Tale of Two Cities* also covers new territory for Dickens as a writer, for it is in this book that the quintessentially British writer leaves London. The novel represents a stylistic break, as well. Around the time he was writing it, Dickens quarreled with the publisher of *Household Words* and founded *All the Year Round*. Dickens seems to have been writing *Two Cities* for the sheer pleasure and interest of it.

The theme was perfect for the time, for the French Revolution fascinated the Victorians. In 1857, while Dickens was recuperating in Brighton from his efforts with "The Frozen Deep," a stage manager by the name of Benjamin Webster read to him "The Dead Heart," a play set during the French Revolution. The ending, in which the hero goes to the guillotine to save the family of the woman he loves, prefigures that of *Two Cities*. Another strong influence at the time was Thomas Carlyle's *The French Revolution* (1837). Carlyle, a prominent historian and social commentator, had been a friend to Dickens for years, and Dickens respected him profoundly. Echoes of Carlyle can be found in Dickens's earlier works, including *Barnaby Rudge* and *Hard Times*. But his influence on *Two Cities* was so strong that Dickens acknowledged it in his preface. Carlyle's history preceded Dickens's novel by some twenty years, and while Dickens was writing Carlyle deluged him with information. Huge passages of Carlyle appear paraphrased in *Two Cities*.

It may be the notion of political unrest that attracted both men to the French Revolution. Both were moderate liberals; they resented the oppression of the common man but feared the consequences of rebellion. Carlyle, who was more moderate than Dickens, resolved this issue in *The French Revolution*: the violence that he depicted was that of a natural disaster. It was horrific, and yet no one person could be blamed. But Dickens's gift lay in humanizing, in sketching moments of compassion or heart in even the bleakest scenes, and in *Two Cities* he made the revolution all about the individual. Dickens's revolutionaries commit atrocities, but they have families; their hands still bloody from slicing throats, they play with their children. Even Charles Darnay, who almost becomes the revolution's victim, is not unsympathetic to the cause.

Dickens was confident of his new creation, his "best story." His public definitely agreed, and the same mobs that had fought for the latest "numbers" of his previous works swarmed the printing house for every chapter. The critical reception was much less enthusiastic. One critic, Sir James Fitzjames Stephen, mocked it in *The Saturday Review* as betraying a fundamental misunderstanding of history, as well as a limited grasp of French—and declared that if Dickens had not been the writer, no one would have bought the book. Chesterton praises the book as "eloquent" but agrees with Stephen that the book is historically biased, that by writing the revolution as he did, Dickens ignored its philosophical and intellectual undercurrents. Even George Bernard Shaw, who defended Dickens's much-maligned *Hard Times* and others for their political value, dismisses *Two Cities* as melodrama.

And the critics have a point. Dickens's France is unconvincing, his Revolution unfair. His Gallic characters are ragged, and his love story flat. The value of the book lies not in its technique, but in its inspiration. It is more poetry than prose, more Dumas than Dickens—a fresh, ruddy, swashbuckling piece from a writer fascinated by the era and alive to its possibilities. And it is the book's final sacrifice that Dickens truly wanted to write: no matter how far a man has fallen, a single selfless act can redeem him.

List of Characters

Charles Darnay is a descendant of the French noble family of St. Evrémonde. Horrified by his family's history of cruelty and repression, he moves to England, changes his name, establishes himself as a teacher of French language and literature, and marries Lucie Manette. He is drawn back to revolutionary France by the appeal of a former servant. There he is captured and sentenced to death as an aristocrat and emigrant by the revolutionary mob. Only the self-sacrifice of a rival suitor of Lucie saves him from the guillotine.

Sydney Carton is a bright but moody and dissipated legal assistant to a successful London lawyer, Mr. Stryver. Unable to win the heart of the woman he loves (Lucie Manette), he leads a life of slovenly despair. He redeems himself finally by giving up his own life so that Lucie's husband, Charles Darnay, might live.

Lucie Manette is the sweet-tempered daughter of Dr. Manette, who was imprisoned in the Bastille for twenty years. When he is rescued, she nurses him back to psychological health. She marries Charles Darnay, with whom she has two children, one of whom dies. It is through love for her that Sydney Carton sacrifices his life to save Charles Darnay.

Dr. Manette is a decent and competent French doctor who is imprisoned in the Bastille for twenty years by the Old Regime. While in prison he learns the craft of shoemaking and writes a detailed account of the cruelties he saw performed by the members of the aristocratic St. Evrémonde family. This account is later used to denounce his own innocent son-in-law, Charles Darnay.

Jarvis Lorry is a fastidious, diplomatic, and well-respected businessman and bachelor. He works for Tellson's, the London bank that handles the accounts of many members of the French aristocracy. He takes Dr. Manette's daughter out of France after her father is imprisoned, later returning to rescue him as well. He remains a close friend of the Manette family and is instrumental in the final rescue of Charles Darnay.

Madame Defarge is the novel's symbol of fate. With her husband she leads the revolutionary movement in Paris from their wineshop. Implacable and relentless, she is consumed by the desire for revenge against the aristocratic regime that tortured and killed members of her family. She compulsively knits a chronicle of the significant events of the Revolution.

Monsieur Defarge is the husband of Madame Defarge, co-owner of the wine-shop, and co-leader of the revolutionary movement in Paris. He is equally unforgiving and even more impatient for revenge than his wife.

The Marquis de St. Evrémonde (Monseigneur), the uncle of Charles Darnay, embodies the vices of the French aristocracy in the eighteenth century. Cruel, selfish, and arrogant, he treats the common people of France like animals. He is assassinated by the father of a peasant child whom he carelessly rode over in his carriage.

Miss Pross is the sturdy and loyal servant of Lucie Manette. She believes that no one is good enough to marry Lucie except her long-lost brother, Solomon, who turns out to be a spy. She kills the fearful Mme. Defarge at the end of the novel.

Solomon Pross/John Barsad is the ne'er-do-well brother of Miss Pross. Her high regard for him notwithstanding, he takes her money, disappears, and reappears years later, first as a spy for the English government, then as a spy for the revolutionary government in France. Carton sees through his double-cross and blackmails him into helping rescue Charles Darnay.

Jerry Cruncher is the rough-hewn messenger and handyman for Tellson's. He moonlights as a "resurrection man"—digging up dead bodies for pay.

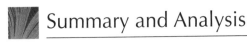

Summary and Analysis

INTRODUCTION

A Tale of Two Cities marks a transition for Dickens, as he began to see the disadvantages of working for others and the advantages of playing by his own rules. It is often thought of as a novel in which he does not "sound like himself"; it is theatrical, melodramatic, often one- or two-dimensional, historically dubious. It ventures away from his well-known London, with mixed results. Even G.K. Chesterton, Dickens's most loyal enthusiast, admits that the novel seems not "entirely by Dickens," that in this instance "the genius of Dickens could not save him" (Chesterton, 100).

Dickens's change of voice was intentional. In his preface, he states his debt to his friend Thomas Carlyle, author of *The French Revolution*. Dickens did not want to achieve here the humanity for which his work was known; he wanted historical sweep, and in that he succeeds. Some of the characters are paper dolls, and almost all are overpowered by the revolutionary backdrop. The gore, or the threat of gore, takes center stage, and at some points the text is more gruesome than is strictly necessary. The strength of the novel lies in its vision; huge in scope and imagination, it does not feel like a series of sketches or vignettes. It is Dickens indulging his lifelong love of the stage.

Just the late date of the novel is remarkable. The novel was first published between 1858 and 1859, when Dickens was on the heels of the masterful *Little Dorrit* and *Bleak House*, and was about to embark upon the enormously satisfying *Great Expectations*. *A Tale of Two Cities* reads like the work of a younger man—idealistic, vehement, inconsistent. While the Dickens of 1858 may not have been a young man, he was changed one. He had left his wife, Catherine Hogarth Dickens, and was rumored to be carrying on an affair with the young actress Ellen Ternan. He had also abandoned his old journal *Household Words* for a new one, *All the Year Round*. His primary inspiration was the role that he had played onstage in "The

Frozen Deep," a play he had coauthored with his friend Wilkie Collins. Richard Wardour of "The Frozen Deep" was a hero to the hilt, an Arctic explorer who sacrifices his life for the rival of the woman that he loves.

A Tale of Two Cities is the work of a man in his second youth, euphemistic for mid-life crisis, a man between families and careers. It represents the altered directions that Dickens was taking as an artist and a man. The doomed romantic hero of whom Dickens had dreamed since "The Frozen Deep" took the form of Sidney Carton—boozy, poor, yet passionate and clever. That Carton was a solicitor's clerk was no random decision; Dickens himself worked as a solicitor's clerk as a young man. In many ways Carton is Charles Dickens as he might have been had he not found success in those critical early years. Unfortunately, the aspect of the book dearest to Dickens's heart—the love triangle Carton forms with Charles Darnay and Lucie Manette—is also its least convincing aspect.

A Tale of Two Cities is a short book, which is perhaps part of the reason why it has been the chosen reading for high school students. But in many ways its brevity makes the novel one of the most difficult of Dickens's books to read. For *Two Cities* may be Dickens's shortest book, but it also covers the longest span of time—seventeen years. It is not just short, it is extraordinarily dense, and in being dense, it is cryptic. Even the chapter titles read like puzzles, "Knitting," for instance, and "The Sea Also Rises." Dickens, who traditionally favored straightforward titles for his novels, here opted for titles that symbolize, rather than summarize, the events.

Most importantly, in his desire to echo Thomas Carlyle's revolutionary history, Dickens sacrificed what he was best at— his characters. "In no other novel," wrote one critic, "has Dickens's natural profusion been so dramatically pruned." (Goldberg, 116) True, he does attempt to dust off a few token personalities—the pompous man-about-town, the kindly clerk, the shrill, yet lovable, spinster—but they feel, ultimately, like stock figures, pale and predictable. Dickens is weary of such figures, and loves them just as little as we do.

In fact, what intrigues us about *A Tale of Two Cities* is not the reasons that usually attract us to its author, but their exact opposite. The character-as-individual, a Dickensian forte, is replaced by the extremely memorable character of the crowd, which "in those times stopped at nothing, and was a monster much dreaded." (Goldberg, 159) Similarly, we do not enjoy *A Tale of Two Cities* for its sentiment, but for its violence. The novel is arguably Dickens's angriest book, angriest because the rage here is without relief. Death and rot run amok on the streets of both London and Paris. Mobs streak their mouths with wine as red as blood; the guillotine slices; flies buzz around crowds hungry for death verdicts in the Old Bailey. Business clerks double as grave robbers, pistols are fired by sweet middle-aged ladies, and every man is corrupt and drinks far too much. And in the distance we hear the relentless click-click of Madame Defarge's knitting needles as she ravels her revenge.

Anger is far from unusual in Dickens, but it is purer in *Two Cities* because there is nothing funny or lovable to distract us from it. More importantly what drives Dickens's other "angry" works—*Bleak House* and *Our Mutual Friend* being perhaps the best examples—is greed. Money is at the root of pestilence and filth. And while greed is a loathsome emotion, it is also rational. The fury in *A Tale of Two Cities* is daemonic; it transcends humanity and human sense like a perverse act of God. Dickens echoes Thomas Carlyle by likening the French Revolution to a natural disaster. For both men, the Revolution is a tumultuous "sea" with spinning whirlpools. Innately violent Mother Nature replaces the civilized order, turning the structured court tribunal into "a jury of dogs empannelled to try a deer." People are wild dogs, flies, and jackals; animals that congregate in swarms and go mad for the scent of blood. For it is blood, that ultimate primal substance, that propels *A Tale of Two Cities*. Dickens is not merely graphic in this novel, he is downright gory. Rent flesh, torn ligaments, dismembered bodies run amok, and he displays an almost unhealthy fascination with executions. His language speaks for itself, suffused as it is with a surgical delight. In one case, a man is half hanged, "sliced down and sliced before his face, and then his inside will be taken out and burnt while he looks on, and then his head will be chopped off and he'll be cut into quarters." In another, a man's "right hand...will be burnt off before his face; that, into wounds which will be made in his arms, his breasts, and his legs, there will be poured boiling oil, melted lead, hot resin, wax, and sulphur; finally he will be torn limb from limb by four strong horses." Dickens, who always excelled in frightening passages, has never been so relentlessly ghoulish. The amount of blood and entrails in a *Tale of Two Cities* rivals that of most horror stories. And his characters are not the recognizable people that usually populate our lives, and indeed, Dickens's own novels; they are the stuff of nightmares, less human beings than they are werewolves, cannibals, and vampires.

BOOK I: RECALLED TO LIFE
Chapter 1 opens in the year 1775, to words that are familiar to all: "It was the best of times, it was the worst of times...." It is a momentous beginning, both sweeping and witty; "we were all going direct to Heaven, we were all going the other way." Certainly it is an uncharacteristic start for an author who usually begins on a note of intimacy. This is not the spirit of Dickens; this is the spirit of Thomas Carlyle, the historian and author of the "wonderful book," *The French Revolution*, that Dickens acknowledges in his preface. The opening chapter is not that of a novel, but of a history; and throughout the novel, the boundary between fact and fiction will be indistinct. Hence, in choosing to begin this way, Dickens reminds us, quite marvelously, of how the best history and the best storytelling can be interchanged.

Dickens may claim that 1775 and 1868 were "so far like," but this is a formality one finds with most historical novels of the time, and in the case of *Two Cities*, it is totally baseless. As we have observed, Dickens is not attracted so much to the similarity between these periods as to the *difference*. The difference affords him a certain amount of creative liberty, for one thing. "There were," he tells us, "a king with a large jaw and a queen with a plain face, on the throne of England." In other Dickens novels, members of royalty enjoy a conspicuous absence, and alone are impervious to his social critique. Dickens had a lot of problems with the systems of his time—he despised the Tory party and attacked them in public more than once—but he adored his queen. Since she was not in power in 1775, though, he can refer to the royalty with all the snideness he desires.

1775 is at odds in other ways with the Victorian turbulence that Dickens usually describes. Indeed, the Industrial and French Revolutions were poles apart. The nineteenth century was powered by greed, desire for productivity, and machines—all of them terrible, but rational and consistent. The 1775 that Dickens paints, on the other hand, is a lunatic era, bipolar with its best and worst, dark and light, a true climate of extremes. Some of Dickens's contemporaries found offense in the liberties he took with this bygone age. One complained, "He takes a sort of pleasure which appears to us insolent and unbecoming to the extreme, in drawing the attention of his readers exclusively to the bad and weak points in the history and character of their immediate ancestors." (Ford, 45) But Dickens is forgiving to eighteenth-century England in the end; if England was wicked, France was much more so. England may have been overrun by people, who, in the words of that same critic, were "a sort of savages...cruel, bigoted, ill-governed, oppressed, and neglected in every way"; but France was a place where a young boy could have his tongue pulled out and be burned to death for neglecting to bow to a local clergyman. According to Dickens, eighteenth-century England was a flawed institution, outdated in some ways, but still with an element of rational consistency; France, on the other hand, is portrayed as a temperamental, dangerous child, and decadent enough to resemble Nero's Rome.

This suits the bipolar nature of Dickens's narrative. In his other books, humor and humanity coexist with trauma. In *A Tale of Two Cities*, however, bloodiness gallops unimpeded by domesticity and tender romance. It helps, therefore, that the author can separate his two narratives by isolating them in his "two cities" of London and Paris. England is familiar, and France is exotic; England is civilized, and France is practically pagan. Hence, The story's conventional elements (love, family, etc.) take place under the British aegis, whereas the new, alien terror is France's alone.

The action launches in **Chapters 2**, **3**, and **4**, as Jarvis Lorry of the venerable Tellson's Bank makes his way to Dover. His coach is stopped en route, and he receives the message "recalled to life"; the meaning of this is clear only to Lorry.

In Dover he meets the young girl Lucie Manette (Chapter 4), at which point the contents of the message are explained. Lucie's father, Dr. Manette, whom Lucie has thought to be dead all these years, is alive. He has been a prisoner in the Bastille for the past twenty years, forsaken by the world. Lucie and Lorry set off for Paris to retrieve him. They find him housed behind a wine shop, where he is cared for by his former servant Defarge, and his wife, who, throughout their interaction, knits and "[sees] nothing." After twenty years of confinement, Dr. Manette has forgotten himself; he believes his name to be that of the cell in which he was imprisoned— One Hundred and Five, North Tower—and compulsively makes shoes. It is up to golden-haired, angelic Lucie to restore him to the man he once was.

It is a queer, almost fairy-tale like tableau in which we find ourselves. Already Paris is distinct in its foreign and dangerous smell; it is a land populated by a gypsy-like woman who knits and says nothing, a banker who talks to phantoms, an old man who sits in the dark dreamily making shoes, and a gang of men who call each other Jacques, so that when they talk, it sounds like they are talking to themselves. ("How goes it, Jacques? Is all the spilt wine swallowed?" "Every drop, Jacques." / "Is it not so, Jacques?" "It is so, Jacques.")

Several elements are at work here, all of them deadly. Man is alone in the world, or, in Dickens's words at the beautiful beginning of Chapter 3, every human creature is a "profound secret and mystery to every other." Moreover, the world in which man finds himself stranded teems with ghosts: "My friend is dead," Dickens laments, "my neighbour is dead, my love, the darling of my soul, is dead." Mr. Lorry's trip to Dover becomes a glum existential road trip, in which he rattles in a carriage completely cut off from the other three who share his coach, deep in conversation with a moldering specter of "cadaverous colour." In *A Tale of Two Cities*, everyday occupations—eating meals, traveling by coach, running a business—become twisted. Even the normally quaint activities of knitting and shoemaking are perverted and take on a sinister air. Perhaps most vivid is the scene that introduces **Chapter 5**, "The Wine Shop": one of the casks has broken, and, in an impromptu revelry, half-starved men, women, and children help themselves. "The wine was red wine, and had stained the ground of the narrow street.... It stained many hands, too, and many faces, and many naked feet, and many wooden shoes." Babies and street sweepers alike gulp at the ominously colored fluid, a portent of the blood in which they will dance for the years to come. That the scene should take place outside the Defarge shop is appropriate, for as we discover, it will be the originator of all bloodshed and madness. The Defarges—who are relatively well off compared to the rest of the oppressed masses—feed those who are hungrier than themselves, and in doing so, train them, like dogs, to attack at their command.

Death and its many variants—disease, insanity, starvation—crowd Book I, but, as befits its title "RECALLED TO LIFE," it is the dynamic between death and life that provides the backbone. All the characters seem to feed on death; and the livelier they are, the more dependent upon death they become. "You'd be in a Blazing bad way if recalling to life was to come into fashion, Jerry!" mutters the messenger to himself at the close of Chapter 2—for, as we learn later, his livelihood depends on those who die and stay dead. The mob outside the wine shop comes to mind; their hunger is not only predatory, it is vampiric. They are dead, at least figuratively so. With their "cadaverous faces," they emerge for the frolic from the "cellars" in which they have been entombed. They are dead until the blood-colored wine revives them. And it is upon these frenzied walking-dead that the Defarges feed. Even amiable Mr. Lorry profits from death, for his employers, Tellson's Bank, make much of their income managing the estates of the deceased. And angelic Lucie Manette's "free...happy" childhood in London is due to her status as an orphan. The only person whose profession involves actually *maintaining* life is the physician Dr. Manette, who starts off Book I as a walking corpse.

The news that Manette is alive is not greeted with joy, but dread. In his daughter Lucie's words, he is "his Ghost!" "I am afraid of it," she shudders, for so thoroughly has Dr. Manette ceased to be a human being. "Recalled to Life" has an ominous, supernatural ring. It implies resurrection, which in such stories often goes wrong. Small wonder that Mr. Lorry finds his mission to France oppressive, for it is a journey "to dig someone out of his grave." Unlike the usual missing person, Dr. Manette cannot be simply found, he must be exhumed. Dickens makes this process as morbid and graphic as possible. The words "Dig, dig, dig," echo through Mr. Lorry's mind as he travels to the Dover Inn, and continue to dog him as he sits by the fire, "digging, digging, digging in the red coals." Retrieving the doctor, therefore, is not unlike robbing a grave. Dickens reinforces this in Chapter 5 when Mr. Lorry and Lucie are finally taken to meet the doctor face to face. They follow the faithful Defarge through a maze that is more tomb than building—an "uncontrollable and hopeless mass of decomposition," "a steep dark shaft of dirt and poison" that is riddled with "spoilt and sickly vapours." The door to Dr. Manette's temporary residence is locked and as heavy as a coffin.

In a book filled with death, Dr. Manette as he appears in **Chapter 6**—though he has a pulse—is at his deadest. For as our hero-martyr Sidney Carton will discover in the end, the actual, physical process of dying can help one pass into immortality—both in Heaven, and also on earth in the hearts of those who remember. The truest death occurs when the world has forgotten one, and one has forgotten oneself, which is the state where we find our Dr. Manette, who knows himself merely as "One Hundred and Five, North Tower." Death is an inevitable part of the resurrection. True, by the end of Book I, it is the living Lucie who restores Manette, but even this is not a simple case of life begetting life. "She laid her head upon my shoulder," Manette babbles, "the night I was summoned out... *Was it you?*" It is not, in fact, Lucie whom Manette sees as he comes out of his trance; rather disturbingly, he confuses his living daughter with the ghost of his dead wife.

Actually, it is not too far-fetched for Manette to make this mistake. Lucie Manette, the heroine in the book, is so angelic she is incorporeal. It is interesting that the "good people"—the ones that Dickens asserts are closest to the living—are practically spectres. Lucie Manette is more spirit than human, her father is a corpse, and Mr. Lorry is a pale composite of all business clerks of Dickens's past, present, and future. The most vital characters are the evil Defarges, especially Madame. Madame may feed on the morbid mayhem and live in a building that smells like the grave, but she is the one character who is truly alive. She teems with sexuality, "with a watchful eye that seldom seemed to look at anything, a large hand heavily ringed, a steady face, strong features, and a great composure of manner." Swathed in furs, with huge earrings and heavy eyebrows; she is gypsy-like. In Book I, she says not a word, and yet she etches herself upon the memory—that of the reader and of the other characters. When Mr. Lorry comes upon the Defarges again fifteen years later in Book III, he recognizes her but not her husband. She is strong, simmering, ripe, and full of blood and heartbeat. Most importantly, she is blessed with a permanent personality; she is unkillable. The men in the wine shop defer to her; indeed, they are both terrified of her and strangely drawn. As we become better acquainted with the Defarges, their marriage reveals itself a masochistic union between a willful man and the one woman who can make him quiver. In fact, Madame Defarge is so central to the bloodshed that it seems impossible to have the French Revolution without her. She is, in fact, modeled on an important Revolutionary figure. Michael Goldberg claims that she originates from Sybil Theroigne, a prostitute who, in Carlyle's account, played an important and vicious Revolutionary role. (Goldberg, 118) The kinship between Theroigne and Madame is fitting. In their own ways, they are both traders of flesh, living off of the blood and desire of their customers.

Though it would be another thirty years before Bram Stoker would publish his *Dracula*, the vampire mythology was already something that was well-cemented in the Victorian imagination. Before Stoker created his Count, vampires were more affiliated with the female personality. The most resonant inspiration was a sixteenth-century Hungarian countess who bathed in the blood of virgins to keep herself young. With all its references to blood, exhumation, and raisings of the dead, *A Tale of Two Cities* is rife with vampiric echoes—and Madame Defarge is its queen. Vampires, in many ways, are more alive than human beings themselves, with their keen senses, their sensuality, and their unquenchable appetites. Madame Defarge nourishes herself on the death of others, she quickens at the smell of blood. As the purveyor of a wine shop, she doles out quantities of that intoxicating, crimson colored drink to the masses, and by doing so, makes them both stronger and enslaves them. Vampire-like, she resurrects human beings in her own image, and ignites them with her hungers and lusts.

BOOK II: THE GOLDEN THREAD

In Book I, Londoners go to Paris; the two cities are apart once again in Book II. Plenty happens in Book II—mysteries, violent death, and rumors of impending massacre are juxtaposed with tranquil interludes of comedy and courtship.

Five years have passed; it is now the year 1780, and we are in London. Back in his own territory, Dickens takes the opportunity to revisit his favorite themes, finance and comedy. Tellson's Bank, the place of Mr. Lorry's employment and where Chapter 1 begins, is well-trodden territory for any reader familiar with Dickens. It is an institution where old men push money and never leave. The Dickens reader is also acquainted with the Punch-and-Judy household of Jerry Cruncher (the mysterious messenger of Book I), which is where the first chapter concludes. Nevertheless, Dickens has not forgotten the roots of his novel. Even at the home of the screwball Crunchers, praying is likened to "flopping" and Jerry Cruncher's son observes that his father's fingers are covered with iron-rust that is the color of dried blood. Meanwhile, Tellson's Bank is a virtual graveyard, and Dickens describes it in terms of decay. It buries its younger employees alive, keeping them "in a dark place, like a cheese" until they have acquired "full Tellson's flavour and a blue mould." Money, estate deeds, and love letters alike are interred in Tellson's in private coffins, "wormy wooden boxes." Livelihoods are not so much nourished here as they are buried, which, as the narrator observes, is not surprising, for "putting to death was a recipe much in vogue."

The English legislation being what it is bodes no good for young Charles Darnay, who stands trial for treason (**Chapters 2–4**). Treason is a particularly scandalous crime that demands a more imaginative justice than mere hanging. As one of the onlookers observes—and we can practically hear him lick his lips as he says it—a man who is condemned for treason is hanged until half-dead, then disemboweled, beheaded, and cut into quarters. So Darnay's is no ordinary trial, and the mob assembled in court is especially keen for conviction. Flies buzz in the Old Bailey, as if, like the crowd, they assume the prisoner is already dead.

As Philip Collins observes in *Dickens and Crime*, the English legal system was never as bad as Dickens, an outspoken opponent of capital punishment, made it out to be. True, England had been governed for many years by what was called the "Bloody Code," under which some two hundred crimes were punishable by death. But, as Collins points out, "The existing court-procedure, too, in some ways favoured the criminal, while juries often quite blatantly reduced the charge on which the prisoners was found guilty, to remove him from danger of the gallows—if, indeed, they did not altogether refuse to convict." (Collins, 4) The bloodlust, the howling

spectators, the unreliable witnesses, the mass condemnations—
even the judges keeling over from time to time from disease
brought by the prisoners—all these things existed, but perhaps
not as ubiquitously as Dickens pretends. Still, his details are
dramatically effective, and build empathy for the accused.

We are convinced of Darnay's innocence by his looks
alone; handsome, and standing erect, he embodies the
Victorian hero. But the judge and the court do not concur, and
the evidence against Darnay is overwhelming. Numerous
witnesses are called for the prosecution. Two of these, the
unsavory John Barsad and Roger Cly, testify to Darnay's
involvement in suspicious activities—traveling between France
and England, meeting with people, and transferring papers, all
of it suggesting conspiracy with the Americans and the French
against the Crown. The other key witnesses are Mr. Lorry and
the Manettes, whom we met in Book I. Lucie is older but even
lovelier; Dr. Manette has recovered his wits; like Mr. Lorry,
they clearly are reluctant to testify. We can assume that both
harbor sympathy for the prisoner Darnay, who, we learn,
chivalrously cared for the ailing Dr. Manette on their journey
back from France five years before. Indeed, their presence is
almost familial, and it comes as a surprise that Darnay and
Lucie are not involved more closely than they are.

The strongest evidence against Darnay is that all his
witnesses identify him beyond a doubt. It is at this point that
Sydney Carton, a clerk for the defense, brilliantly steps in:
having obscured his face until now, he rises to reveal that he
and Darnay are almost identical. It is a fatal blow to the
prosecution, and Darnay is acquitted—or, as Jerry Cruncher
mumbles, "[r]ecalled to life." In barely escaping execution,
Darnay shares a kinship with Dr. Manette; like Manette, he has
been brought back from the dead. His release is much to the
sorrow of the bloodthirsty crowd, and Dickens somewhat
cynically entitles this chapter "A Disappointment."

Darnay's acquittal is a bit disappointing logically, too. He
escapes conviction by the improbable coincidence that he looks
exactly like the defense clerk—which in itself explains nothing.
Darnay clearly *did* make the mysterious passage between Dover

and Calais that the prosecution accuses him of; the Manettes establish that. And his effect on Dr. Manette is troubling: at one point, his face "[becomes] frozen, as it were, in a very curious look at Darnay: an intent look, deepening into a frown of dislike and distrust, not even unmixed with fear." The nature and true extent of Darnay's involvement in—whatever he has been involved in—is not a point the book resolves.

In another Victorian's work, Darnay would have been the hero of the tale. He is good-looking and pure of intent, and the angelic heroine supports him. But the Charles Dickens who wrote *A Tale of Two Cities* was no longer interested in pretty, upstanding young men, a position he made apparent in *Bleak House* by killing off the golden-haired lover Richard Carstone. What seems to attract the mature Dickens is not the *born* hero, but the flawed man who earns the title. Sidney Carton is the diligent and gifted law clerk for Darnay's defense, and Darnay's twin and savior; he also is cynical, strange, morose, self-absorbed, and so roundly disliked as to be wanted only where he works. But he is the protagonist, and will become the hero.

Mr. Stryver, once Carton's colleague and now his boss, is a rotund lawyer with ambitions to match his name. The two men push papers together and drink through the night. Theirs is a dim, corrupt, and filthy environment, but the only place in which Carton belongs, for Stryver recognizes his talents. Stryver sees himself as the lion, and Carton as "The Jackal" (**Chapter 5**); Stryver works little and walks grandly in the sun, while Carton nimbly chases scraps in the dark. Though surely more talented than Stryver, Carton lacks social graces and the taste for glory, and will never match Stryver's success.

Carton is a drowning man, the kind that the hero of an earlier novel might be cautioned to avoid. It is not surprising, then, that Darnay seems uncomfortable around him. Already Carton has been a savior twice—when Lucie faints in court, it is Carton who catches her and prevents her being trampled by the Old Bailey crowd—but he is anything but gracious about Darnay's gratitude. The two men dine together after the trial, but Carton's uncivil behavior leads Darnay to leave him in the tavern, where Carton orders a bottle and a wake-up call. He recognizes Darnay's discomfort, and he matches it with envy: "Come on! And have it out in plain words," he tells himself. "You hate the fellow."

Carton's ministrations to Lucie go unacknowledged because she is already so full of affection for Darnay. And so she should be; he is noble and sweet, whereas Carton is a wastrel and a drunkard. And who can blame Carton for resenting Darnay? Though Carton has proven his ingenuity and has been of service to the Manettes twice, and looks just like Darnay, Darnay is his social superior. Darnay probably will go on to a conventionally happy future with Lucie, but Carton foresees no future whatsoever for himself. Darnay seems to lack the acute self-awareness that is Carton's burden.

Chapter 6 finds us at the home of the Manettes, four months later. Just as Paris and London are distinct in the novel, so are the worlds of business and hearth; the Manette home is a cool, pleasing retreat in Soho, "a very harbour from the raging streets," far from problems of money and law. This will be the last scene set in England for a while, and it serves two functions: it is a "roll call" for the important British players, and it leaves us with a gentler impression of England than Dickens has given us so far.

The Manettes lead a modest life. Together with her aging father, Lucie lives the sort of demure existence that befits most Dickensian heroines. Indeed, that quintessential quality of feminine thrift that Dickens so often exalts is obvious in the Manette home; its little mistress has the "ability to make much of little means," and the dinner she provides is equally frugal and agreeable. Mr. Lorry is first to appear, for he has become a family friend. Also present is Miss Pross, who flew through in Book I; here we are told that the irascible spinster was hired by Tellson's to raise the orphaned Lucie. There is Lucie herself, golden and quiet, with her father, the doctor, who has recovered his mind. Also on the scene, though less explicably, is Charles Darnay. Sidney Carton "lounge[s] in" later, in time for tea. Even Jerry Cruncher makes a brief appearance, as he shows up to escort Mr. Lorry back to his quarters. As pleasant as this evening seems, it ends with a warning; rain begins to fall, and the patter of drops against the roof sounds like the footsteps of "hundreds of people." Even as they sit safe in Soho, they seem to hear their happy home besieged by the multitudes. The chapter ends with a "memorable storm," with "not a moment's interval in crash, and fire, and rain" until its end.

By the close, the relationships among these characters are fixed. Mr. Lorry is fond of the Manettes, as they are of him. Miss Pross has two passions in her life: for her absent brother Solomon, who seems to have taken her money and abandoned her on a street corner, and for Lucie, whom she adores ferociously enough to declare Lucie's own father unworthy of the girl's love. Charles Darnay loves Lucie, and we can assume they are on track for marriage. Dr. Manette loves Lucie and *likes* Charles Darnay—though, truth be told, something about Darnay makes him afraid. In this scene, for instance, Darnay offers a simple story about a discovery made in the Tower of London: "Upon the corner stone in an angle of the wall," he tells Manette, "one prisoner, who seemed to have gone to execution, had cut as his last work, three letters...DIG." Darnay goes on to explain that papers had been hidden beneath, at which point Lucie exclaims, "My father, you are ill!" Manette "recover[s] himself almost instantly," but Lorry notices "on his face, as it turned towards Charles Darnay, the same singular look that had been upon it when it turned towards him in the passages of the Court House." It is that same "intent look, deepening into a frown of dislike and distrust, not even unmixed with fear."

Sidney Carton loves Lucie, but hopelessly. In fact, no one particularly likes Sidney; they put up with him because he saved Darnay. He may be a "jackal," but not by choice. As he says about Charles Darnay, "I should have been much the same sort of fellow, if I had had luck." He is a "man of good abilities and good emotions" but incapable "of his own help and his own happiness." In short, he is a jackal by profession but not by nature; unlike the London and Paris masses, he is not sustained by blood and filth. Rather, he is "like one who died young."

Had Dickens not professed such tenderness for his hero, we might not have guessed that he identified with him. Sidney—one of Dickens's many nicknames from childhood—is one of the author's queerest personas. He is not like David Copperfield, a talented boy who, with the help of fate, rescues himself from obscurity. Like Copperfield, Dickens was lucky. In his youth he clerked for a lawyer's office, plagued by the family debt that had sent his father to prison more than once. He believed himself doomed to a life of drudgery. Carton is Dickens without the luck, Dickens as he might have been, noble of spirit but thwarted by the world.

Despite his luck, though, at the time of *Two Cities* Dickens was feeling just as lost. By his forties, he had achieved success, but he was miserable. It seems to have been a kind of "midlife crisis"; he had children, the house he'd always wanted, a wife he didn't love, and fame that no longer excited them. Since acting in "The Frozen Deep," Dickens had been fascinated by the scoundrel-martyr figure, and Carton seems an expression and exploration of that—an antisocial, self-destructive, persistently dramatic character who somehow ultimately finds redemption.

Chapter 7 finds us back in Paris, but a very different Paris from the one we left at the close of Book I. This is the Paris of the aristocrats on the eve of their destruction, and Dickens's opulent depiction of this world is a joy. We find ourselves in a world that we can liken to decadent Rome, a wasteful place where our first Monseigneur—one of many people called "Monseigneur" in the novel, the word being French for "my lord"—requires four attendants to administer his morning cup of chocolate, and where even the executioner is puffed, powdered, frilled, and beribboned. But the pace quickens as this Monseigneur and his company depart, leaving behind another Monseigneur, "Monsieur the Marquis"—later revealed to be Darnay's uncle, the lord of the St. Evrémonde family.

The Marquis is "a man of about sixty, handsomely dressed, haughty in manner, and with a face like a fine mask," though his nostrils "give a look of treachery, and cruelty, to the whole countenance." Whereas the rest of his class is silly, he is scornful and arrogant. He is also a sociopath who sees cruelty as entertainment. He despises his own class, but he can only unleash his hatred on those who cannot fight back, which he does with abandon. We find him crashing through the streets in his carriage, whipping his horses to a froth and terrifying pedestrians; finally he runs over a child. "It is extraordinary to me," he tells the crowd that gathers at the scene, "that you people cannot take care of yourselves and your children. One or the other of you is for ever in the way. How do I know what injury you have done my horses?" He tosses out a gold coin in compensation for the father's loss.

Here Dickens starkly paints the classes that will soon be at war. Defarge appears and is made way for, and he offers superficial comfort to the father: "It is better for the poor little plaything to die so, than to live. It has died in a moment without pain. Could it have lived an hour as happily?" It is a poor argument for a grieving parent, and its larger purpose is clear: it is political speech. One man's tragedy is another's example, and, however subtly, Defarge is recruiting.

The Marquis's level of awareness is unclear, though his smile suggests he does not appreciate the deeper meaning. The coin he tosses to Defarge is to reward him for being a "philosopher"—for knowing his place. And in this he and Defarge, and the people like them, are similar: each side is capable of dehumanizing, of stripping the significance from death. The same lack of empathy that has created the disparity between classes soon will be working to end it.

Chapter 8 shows us "Monseigneur in the Country." A village in his domain is poor to the point of destitution—"life on the lowest terms that could sustain it"—but he continues to tax its inhabitants without mercy. The villagers eat onions and wild leaves for dinner. There are "no children" on the streets, no growth or joy. A peasant woman pleads with him to allow "a morsel of stone or wood" to mark her husband's grave, a request that the Marquis does not even acknowledge. The woman's speech to him is important, for she describes at length the suffering in the area. We cannot defend the Marquis as uninformed.

But the Marquis's villainy will in fact not go unavenged. The dead child's father has ridden home with him, clinging to the bottom of his carriage.

Before the father's vengeance can be wrought, though, the Marquis has an appointment for dinner with his nephew, Charles Darnay (**Chapter 9**). Now that we know that Darnay and this callous man are related, we can begin to understand why Darnay makes Dr. Manette recoil. Charles Darnay may have a noble soul, but he comes from corrupt roots. The son of the Marquis's twin brother, he is the only surviving heir to the family property. Relations between uncle and nephew are strained; Charles has stirred up trouble for the family, and the Marquis has attempted to put him into prison. Now Charles rejects the family name as shameful and refuses to assume his place as heir; he prefers his penniless English life to the decadence of the Marquis.

The next morning, the Marquis lies dead, stabbed through the heart with a knife that bears a message: "Drive him fast to his tomb. This, from JACQUES." Jacques is the name that Monsieur Defarge shares with his colleagues at the wine shop. From Paris, then, the Defarges have managed to scheme Marquis's death. The actual assassin was Gaspard, the grieving father whom Defarge recruited so subtly in Chapter 7. In death, the Marquis is very much as he was in life. Living, he was like a "stone face" on a rich façade, "handsomely diabolic." Dead, his face is "like a fine mask, suddenly startled, made angry, and petrified"—startled and angry, presumably, that anyone should take away the life and fortune he considered his hereditary right. The title of this chapter is "The Gorgon's Head," referring to the chiseled faces on the exterior of the château; death, like a gorgon, has petrified the marquis and added his face to the others.

Dickens carries the distinction between his "two cities" to the language itself—a technique he often employs in his novels. His most street-trodden characters speak in the Queen's tongue as if to signify an inherent gentility. In *A Tale of Two Cities*, this technique serves a slightly different end. Dickens's francophones are automatically suspect; they speak as if their words had been translated crudely. The Defarges and the Marquis speak French at its most stilted, for an effect which, as a contemporary critic observed, "for a few sentences, is amusing enough, but which becomes intolerably tiresome and affected." (Ford, 43) "But you must be fatigued," the Marquis tells his nephew. "Shall we terminate our conference for the night?" Charles's French is no less affected. "I know," he says, "that your diplomacy would stop me by any means, and would not scruple as to means." The minute that Charles Darnay is back in England, the effect disappears. He speaks only pure English, even with his compatriots the Manettes. He has embraced England fully and taken on its words, abandoning as far as possible his French origins.

A year passes, and Darnay has abandoned the château that is rightfully his and established himself in England as, of all things, a language tutor. After a year of honest work, he has finally plucked up the courage to ask for Lucie's hand in marriage. Despite Manette's reluctance to let Lucie go, he has no choice but to accept a proposal from such a fine suitor. He promises to praise Darnay to Lucie if she should ask about him. Darnay wishes to confess his Evrémonde origins, but Manette stops him; he will accept confessions only if the courtship is successful, only on the wedding day. These are the "Two Promises" of **Chapter 10**: Manette will speak highly of Darnay to his daughter, and Darnay will not reveal his secret until the wedding day. The chapter closes with a prophetic relapse, as Manette returns to making shoes.

The episode in which Mr. Stryver courts Lucie (**Chapters 11 and 12**) is a comic interlude. Stryver, with his big belly, his port, and his delusions of grandeur, is a silly man who sees himself as a lion when he is more of a baboon. In wooing Lucie, he is a type, a suitor who is blind to the obvious—the grotesque difference in age, temperament, and physique. "It will be a piece of good fortune for her," Stryver claims, "but she deserves a good fortune." Carton, his confidant, diverts Stryver to Mr. Lorry, to whom falls the thankless task of diplomatically crushing Stryver's hopes. He hints that Miss Manette may have other affections; Stryver scoffs. Lorry suggests that he act as emissary. In the end, Lorry triumphs, and Stryver takes his leave, scorning "the mincing vanities and giddiness of empty-headed girls," and magnanimously wishing, though not predicting, that Lucie will not end in poverty and regret. This is the only moment of *A Tale of Two Cities* when the grimness is completely absent. When Mr. Lorry comes to him with news from the Manettes, far from being the longing lover, Stryver is already heavy at the drink and at his paperwork—and Lorry has to work even to raise the subject in conversation. Stryver seems to have forgotten her entirely. At the moment, Lucie's heart simply is not relevant.

Sidney Carton's declaration of love to Lucie Manette in **Chapter 13** solidifies the romantic triangle central to the novel. It is already understood by now that Lucie and Darnay love each other, and that it will not be long before they are married. But Carton comes to Lucie with a suit of his own—that he should be allowed to pledge his life to her, not as a husband, but as the guardian of her happiness. Although Darnay gets the girl, Dickens does not allow Darnay a sweeping proposal scene. It is Carton who gets the lover's limelight, and of the two declarations of love, his is by far the stronger.

For Carton, Lucie transcends earthly love. In her he has found inspiration. She makes him young and hopeful once more. When she is present, he hears "old voices impelling [him] upward, that [he] thought were silent for ever" and has "unformed ideas of striving afresh, beginning anew." He has begun to think of redemption. Lucie hears his confession "pale and trembling" and weeps for him; she vows to believe that he loves her, though he admits he is unworthy of her. His "last supplication" to her is that she "[t]ry to hold [him] in [her] mind, at some quiet times, as ardent and sincere in this one thing"—that she remember him, when he has returned to his vices, in this one moment of worthiness. The end of the scene tells us clearly where the author's interest lies: Carton finishes his monologue, says goodbye, blesses Lucie, and exits, and no reaction from the beloved is shown.

Such a long duration at the Manette home has made us forget the grime of London that exists outside their door. Therefore, it is with some kind of relief that we find ourselves booted out of the Manette Soho residence and onto the street (**Chapter 14**). We are outside the sooty façade of Tellson's Bank, where Mr. Jerry Cruncher sits with his son, observing a funeral. Thank heavens for Jerry Cruncher, who, until now, has not been given the chance to shine. His humor—the grim, graveyard, gritty humor—seems much more in accordance with the mood of *Two Cities*.

At the moment, life for Cruncher is hard. There are not enough tasks at Tellson's, and there is not enough custom in the streets. Jerry's wife, much to his annoyance, is still "flopping," his graphic description of praying. So Cruncher turns to his real trade—grave robbing. It explains the rust that clings to his knuckles like dried blood, for coffin locks are rusty. He calls himself a "Resurrection-Man," contributing to the cause of science through all the corpses he sells to doctors.

Dickens loves Cockneys, with their grime, their "Hoor-rars," their eccentricities. Cruncher is the strongest comic character in *Two Cities*, and Dickens enjoys him: "Time was, when a poet sat upon a stool in a public place, and mused in the sight of men. Mr. Cruncher, sitting on a stool in a public place, but not being a poet, mused as little as possible, and looked about him." Perhaps Cruncher works because he touches the same graveyard sensibility that most attracts us to *Two Cities*. He is a coffin robber covered in dried rust who beleaguers his wife, watches for funerals, and makes the rest of his income shuttling elderly wealthy ladies with one foot in the grave. He is far more a jackal than Carton could ever be, for he really does live off of the dead. But this chapter's comedy also works because it is honest. Cruncher may prey on the dead and dying and abuse his "missus," but there is no hypocrisy in him. Indeed, he believes that his "resurrection" work is a decent calling; he is a purveyor, as he explains, "in a branch of Scientific goods."

His son is his reflection. Little Jerry fits the Dickens old-man-as-little-child mold; his forebears are Dick Swiveller from

The Old Curiosity Shop and the Artful Dodger of Oliver Twist. He is wise and street-bitten but still innocent and forward-thinking. He believes in the power of money and the rewards of hard work. Most importantly, he believes in his father. Because Jerry Senior is honest, he will be able to redeem himself in the end, and we get a hint of that at the end of the chapter. Jerry, after an evening of digging up graves, walks away with a son who looks up to him. "Oh, father," he says, "I should so like to be a Resurrection-Man when I'm quite growed up!" It is a quaint, morbid, hysterical scene, but also a touching one. "[T]here's hopes wot that boy will yet be a blessing to you!" Cruncher grunts to himself. Cruncher may make his living from corpses, but he has a responsibility toward life, at least to the life of his son. And he is slouching, slowly, toward meeting that responsibility.

The funeral that Cruncher observes, incidentally, is that of Roger Cly, one of the men who testified against Charles Darnay in court, and by profession an "old Bailey spy." The same night, the younger Cruncher follows his father to the graveyard as he goes to plunder Cly's coffin. When he finally catches up to his father, however, he finds Jerry disgruntled and empty-handed.

In Paris, the mood is gloomy. People are drinking earlier than usual, but unfortunately the wine that they imbibe is "unusually thin" and "souring," just like the blood that throbs in their veins. "No vivacious Bacchanalian flame leaped out of the pressed grape," writes Dickens in **Chapter 15**. Wine is useless; only gore can cheer these people up. Fortunately, Defarge arrives with a road-mender from the countryside, who revitalizes them with his tale of the Marquis's death and the subsequent execution of his killer, who is left "hanging, poisoning the water." But what is most memorable is the way in which the Defarges turn this road-mender—whom they have re-christened as Jacques Five—into their acolyte. So far, this is the most tantalizing glimpse into how the Defarges consolidate their power. They take him to welcome the king and queen of France, whereupon the road-mender finds himself overcome by an urge to join the infectious worship. Instead of scolding him, the Defarges encourage his embarrassing, slobbering show. "Judiciously show a cat milk," Defarge explains, "if you wish to make her thirst for it. Judiciously show a dog his natural prey, if you wish for him to bring it down one day."

The Defarges not only understand a crowd, they know how to manipulate it—through its hunger. In some ways, they are just as contemptuous of the common man as was the Marquis. The difference is that they know better how to use the common man. Defarge is like a breeder of attack dogs—he whets the people's appetites, but instead of starving them, as the Marquis does, he feeds them, and in doing so, trains them to kill on his command. It makes him a spectacular oligarch. His men not only follow him, they take a new name— Jacques—perhaps the most fundamental demonstration of servility. The road-mender is the fifth Jacques to join Defarge's circle. Like the Jacques before him, he relinquishes his identity, and becomes, in essence, Defarge's ideological son. Who he once was has ceased to exist; what exists now is whatever man whom Defarge wants him to be.

This makes Madame Defarge all the more powerful—for if the men bow to Defarge, he in turn bows to her. Every member of the Defarge gang is haunted by a "mysterious dread of madame." Yet dread makes her all the more attractive. The road-mender finds himself glancing constantly her way. More importantly, Madame Defarge wields her power without a word. It is only at the close of Chapter 15 that she actually speaks. "You work hard, madame," says someone; "Yes," she replies; "I have a good deal to do."

Rather than talk, Madame Defarge knits. Among other things, she knits "shrouds" and a "register" of grievances to be redressed, murders to be avenged, and names to remember. Above all, she knits the future. Every click of her needles is another person, another fate. Her knitting aligns her with several goddess-figures, particularly the Fates, who spin the threads of life to snip at their will.

It is by choice that Madame remains taciturn. As a goddess, she transcends the everyday banality of verbal exchange. When she does speak at length, it is to indoctrinate, as gradually as necessary. An exchange with the road-mender:

> ... [Y]ou would shout and shed tears for anything, if it made a show and a noise. Say! Would you not?"
>
> "Truly, madame, I think so. For the moment."
>
> "If you were shown a great heap of dolls, and were set upon them to pluck them to pieces and despoil them for your own advantage, you would pick out the richest and gayest. Say! Would you not?"
>
> "Truly yes, madame."
>
> "Yes. And if you were shown a flock of birds, unable to fly, and were set upon them to strip them of their feathers for your own advantage, you would set upon the birds of the finest feathers; would you not?"
>
> "It is true, madame."
>
> "You have seen both dolls and birds to-day," said Madame Defarge, with a wave of her hand towards the place where they had last been apparent; "now, go home!"

Her argumentation rivals any at the Old Bailey, and the effect is as damning.

As a rule the only person whom Madame converses with is her husband. Defarge may seem like a god to the hordes he commands, but he is in actuality a mere high priest. He is Madame's mouthpiece, and her medium to the world. The philosophies he spouts—for Defarge is an eloquent and sometimes long-winded man—are of her origination. Like a god to a priest, she communicates to him alone and in private. It is in their scenes together that the formidable Monsieur Defarge seems fallible. His typical pose before her when they talk is with bent head, and clasped hands, "like a docile and attentive pupil before his catechist." As all deities before her, Madame Defarge's goals are grand; in this case, her goal is the extermination of the aristocratic race. Being mortal, Monsieur Defarge worries about the time and effort such a goal will take. Being immortal, Madame Defarge does not.

Madame does not only highlight Defarge's weakness; she also brings out his humanity. For instance, she compels him to confess his sympathy for Charles Darnay. Darnay, as the nephew of the late Marquis, is the last surviving member of the family that, for some yet-unknown reason, Madame has pledged to annihilate. But Darnay is to marry Lucie Manette, and Defarge still feels loyal to Dr. Manette, who was once his employer. "I hope," he ventures, "for her sake, Destiny will keep her husband out of France." And his secondary position suits him; he admires his wife. "A great woman," he declares as he watches her move about the evening street, making contacts with other women—for like the rest of the men in the wine shop, he delights in observing her unawares—"a strong woman, a grand woman, a frightfully grand woman!"

Madame and Monsieur Defarge are stereotypically Gallic. They are powerful, fleshy, passionate—and linked to the Frenchest of all things, wine. Along those lines, their union is the perfect French marriage. Alone, Monsieur Defarge is a strong man, one who excels at forming a posse and leads the invasion upon the Bastille. He is "a strongly-made man" but not as memorable as he would like to be. There is almost a wistfulness in the way that Defarge tries to tout his own importance, "My name is Defarge," he tells Charles Darnay, "and I keep a wine-shop in the Quartier Saint Antoine. Possibly you have heard of me." For Defarge always pales in comparison to his wife. Mr. Lorry senses this. "Do I know you?" he asks Monsieur, whereas he recognizes Madame Defarge—with whom he has never exchanged a word—instantly. When the Defarges are together, he diminishes even more, becoming "reserved...mechanical." Even the mention of the word "wife" has a spell on him. Charles Darnay's innocent remark, "My wife came to your house...?" is more damaging than Darnay knows. For Defarge, though terrible, is on verge of pitying the son-in-law of his former master. But Darnay's reference to "wife" reminds Defarge of his servitude to his own spouse. "The word ... seemed to serve as a gloomy reminder to Defarge," who immediately turns back to being cold and officious. Defarge controls the people, Madame controls Defarge. Among his own flock, he wields seemingly god-like power; with her, however, he is a chastened little boy. But Defarge does not resent her for being more powerful than himself; he loves her and her domineering ways. He literally trembles—out of both fear and lust—in her presence.

His admiration closes **Chapter 16**, much of which his wife spends reassuring him that their efforts have not been in vain:

> "It does not take a long time," said madame, "for an earthquake to swallow a town. Eh well! Tell me how long it takes to prepare the earthquake?"
>
> "A long time, I suppose," said Defarge.
>
> "But when it is ready, it takes place, and grinds to pieces everything before it. In the meantime, it is always preparing, though it is not seen or heard."

In this chapter, we learn that the spy Barsad is in the neighborhood; Defarge describes him so thoroughly for his wife's register that she actually laughs.

We also see the almost military manner in which Madame runs the wine shop. She manages the money, the customers, and the "serving man," just as she manages her husband's flagging spirits. She is a watcher; her eye misses nothing.

When Barsad appears and tries to seduce the Defarges into saying something incriminating, Madame's careful management thwarts him. His only "hit" is Defarge's reaction to the news that Lucie will marry Darnay, the nephew of the late Marquis. Madame adds Darnay's name to the register after Barsad's.

It is worth noting that when Barsad greets Defarge as "Jacques," Defarge denies the name. His name is Ernest. The "Jacquerie" are men who have re-baptized themselves, joining a brotherhood.

We return to London for Lucie Manette and Charles Darnay's wedding (**Chapters 17–20**). Lucie and Charles's courtship is conspicuously absent from the story—remarkable, considering the Victorian reader's lust for romance. Like the lovers themselves, the wedding proves to be sweet, modest, and passionless. Joyful tears sparkle as prettily as jewels, the bride's dress is demure, and the only guests are the faithful Mr. Lorry and Miss Pross. The only hint of unease comes from Dr. Manette. Many affectionate fathers may have qualms about releasing their daughter to another man, but Dr. Manette seems unusually distraught. He ruminates about his time in prison, and tells Lucie how she haunted him there. He babbles about his old cravings for vengeance. He seems less like a joyful father of the bride, and more like a man in turmoil. On the wedding day, Charles Darnay fulfills the pledge he made to Manette when he asked his permission to marry Lucie, by revealing his true identity, which we already know: he is the current Marquis St. Evrémonde. The shock drives the doctor back to his former state of disorder. As soon as the newlyweds depart for their honeymoon, he becomes a shoemaker once more.

The doctor's response to Darnay's news is just one in a string of unexplained mysteries in this book. *A Tale of Two Cities* has much in common with the horror story, but it also has many elements of a detective novel, a genre which is much indebted to Dickens's friend Wilkie Collins, author of *The Moonstone* and *The Woman in White*, as well as "The Frozen Deep." Dickens was not new to introducing mystery in his novels; unknown parentage was one of his favorite topics. But in most of his books, the mysteries are usually limited to one, to which we generally guess the solution. In contrast, *A Tale of Two Cities* is packed with questions, all of them bewildering: Why is John Barsad in France? Where is Roger Cly's body? Where is Miss Pross's oft-mentioned absent brother, Solomon? The central mystery, however, involves the St. Evrémonde family, and why they are so universally despised. Darnay changed his name to leave them behind, Madame Defarge calls for their extermination, and the very mention of their name is enough to drive Dr. Manette mad. Like the classic "whodunnit," *A Tale of Two Cities* is strewn with clues, but the answers do not appear until the very end.

For nine days Dr. Manette resumes his cobbler guise, becoming more shoemaker than doctor with each passing day—"growing dreadfully skillful ... intent on his work ... so nimble and expert." In this novel, the doctor's shoemaking bears an uncanny resemblance to knitting. It relieves pain, explains Dr. Manette later, "by substituting the perplexity of the fingers for the perplexity of the brain," in short, it is a mechanical activity, like knitting, to keep desires and memories at bay.

On the tenth day, Dr. Manette recovers, although he remembers nothing of the preceding nine days. He is also bewildered as to what might have triggered his behavior. It seems as though the Doctor's sanity depends on forgetfulness. With this in mind, Mr. Lorry persuades him to burn his shoemaker's bench, Manette's "old companion." The bench is a memento from Manette's past, but he cannot part with it; he needs reassurance that it will be there if his pain returns. Nevertheless, we are not entirely sure that destroying the bench, which Mr. Lorry does with Miss Pross and without the doctor, is the best solution. After all, Dr. Manette cannot be completely cured if he neglects rather than confronts his demons. Dickens's language is suitably admonitory. First, by personifying the bench as an "old companion," he likens its destruction to murder. Once in the hands of Miss Pross and Mr. Lorry, it becomes a "body" which is hacked apart and burnt, and its accessories, the shoemaker's tools, are buried in the garden. Though Mr. Lorry and Miss Pross are not aware of the ramifications of their act, they are uneasy. "[They] almost felt, and almost looked, like accomplices in a horrible crime."

With the return of the newlyweds, life resumes its happy pace. The only possible blemish is Sidney Carton, who asks Darnay's permission to spend a few evenings in the household. Darnay agrees, but not without reluctance. To his wife and in-laws, he mocks Carton, and speaks lightly of his failures. It is up to Lucie, with all her sweetness, to reprimand her husband for his lack of compassion, and to invite Carton in. She continues, however, to guard her own secret with Carton.

The first half of **Chapter 21**, "Echoing Footsteps," chronicles the family harmony that continues unimpeded for the next six years. Lucie has two children. Doctor Manette cures patients. Mr. Lorry visits, and Miss Pross fusses over the expenses. Sidney Carton is a guest also, coming four or five times a year; and if he goes largely unacknowledged by the adults, he has found adoration in Lucie's infants. The one nuisance is Mr. Stryver, who marries a wealthy widow, spawns three healthy brats, and hires Darnay to tutor them. In this Soho residence, calamity is impossible. It is a protected house, a house of "echoes"—history, madness, and starving crowds may resound here from time to time, but they are harmless, glancing shadows.

Indeed, in all of London, tranquility reigns. This London is in marked contrast to the London of the book's beginning, where crowds hanker for executions, spies abound, and honest men exhume corpses. Here, Dickens's patriotism may be getting the better of him. He introduces London on a sinister note but does not have the heart to sustain it. After all, *A Tale of Two Cities* is premised on good English people and vicious French ones; hence, London, in the second half of the book, is more idyllic than any London that Dickens has ever written. The London of the Old Bailey and Tellson's Bank and graveyards is far away, and the Soho house ceases to be a refuge from the city, and becomes representative, a homespun place where virtue reigns and tragedy is unheard-of. "Even when there were sounds of sorrow among the rest," Dickens writes, "they were not harsh and cruel." Even the death of Lucie's son is unexpectedly idyllic:

Even when golden hair, like her own, lay in a halo on a pillow round the worn face of a little boy, and he said, with a radiant smile, "Dear papa and mamma, I am very sorry to leave you both, and to leave my pretty sister; but I am called, and I must go!" those were not tears all of agony that wetted his young mother's cheek, as the spirit departed from her embrace that had been entrusted to it. Suffer them and forbid them not. They see my Father's face. O Father, blessed words!

Lucie's dead son is not mentioned again in the book.

Perhaps this is why the second half of "Echoing Footsteps" is so enjoyable. Dickens, who has kept his two cities apart for so long, starts to draw them together. "Echoing Footsteps" is the one and only chapter in which both cities star side by side. And what a contrast it is! It is, after all, the year 1789. At the same time peace reigns in Soho, in Paris the Bastille is being stormed. The onslaught is magnificent. Men and women swarm carrying knives.

History tells us that those who were truly responsible for the Revolution were not the people nominally in charge, but local groups of working-class people, called "les sans-culottes," with their individual leaders. (Barzun, 427) And the Revolution does seem impossible without the Defarges. In the Bastille scene, fiction mixes with history, with the Defarges at the head of one of the most powerful local groups; indeed, it almost seems that the Defarges alone are responsible for this monumental event. Heads are severed and put on pikes; chambers are burned. By the end of the siege, seven prisoners are freed, and seven heads of guards line the walls, impaled on sticks. But the goriest moment belongs to Madame Defarge, who actually hacks off the head of a Bastille guard with a kitchen knife. Monsieur's duties are comparatively bureaucratic. While his wife slices, he has a task that takes him into the cell formerly occupied by Dr. Manette.

The Bastille is just the beginning, however, and its violent ecstasy carries us into **Chapter 22**, where an old aristocrat by the name of Foulon is discovered hiding in a government building. This is where the women—Madame's army—are truly allowed to shine. "The men were terrible, in the bloody-minded anger with which they looked from the windows ... but the women were a sight to chill the boldest." At this point another woman is introduced. Dubbed "the Vengeance" by her comrades, she is Madame Defarge's companion in arms. Surely she is qualified for this lofty title, for she herself is more demon than either human or beast. The "plump wife of a starved grocer," she has kept her figure in meager times by feeding off her husband.

What follows is a Bacchanal in the truest sense; like the followers of Dionysus, god of wine and madness, women swarm into the streets, beating their breasts, tearing their hair, and chanting their grievances, each eager to descend upon her victim and tear him limb from limb. "Rend Foulon to pieces, and dig him into the ground, that grass may grow from him!" they call. And like the Bacchae, they dance until some of them swoon from ecstasy. The aristocrat Foulon and his son-in-law are scratched and screeched at, and then finally lynched by Madame Defarge. Their bodies are then ripped apart, and heads and hearts paraded on a pike.

The events being depicted here represent a breakdown of one social order and the emergence of another, one that has been building in strength over time—but, as Madame Defarge predicted, the change is sudden and violent, like a storm. As opposed to the British religion of calm and order, even in the courts, France's revolution has a distinctly pagan feel.

Indeed, we almost wonder again whether we are in eighteenth-century France or ancient Rome. There are parallels between French and Roman history. Imperial Rome fell, and was reborn as a Republic. Both Republics came under the rule of men, Julius Caesar and Napoleon, respectively, who then reinstated imperial rule. It was something that French leaders themselves were well aware of. In the words of Simon Schama, "The French Revolution was obsessed with the model of the Roman Republic in particular." (169) Moreover, as Schama points out, the French leaders found parallels with the regime that they sought to overcome. In that historian's words, "...the stereotypes of the age in which they lived corresponded to the worst excesses of gilded corruption decried in the Roman histories." (170) Dickens plays on this relationship throughout the book. Early on, he likens aristocratic France to

Imperial Rome in its decadence. Later, he calls a wine shop "The Good Republican Brutus of Antiquity." As Brutus was the man who murdered Caesar in order to preserve the Republic, his name was probably quite popular—quite possibly a good luck charm.

But Dickens's revolutionary France is Roman in other ways as well, for it has a distinct pagan and Bacchanalian flavor. By focusing on this, Dickens fails us as a historian. Behind the Revolution, there was Roman-derived madness and Roman-derived reason; Dickens ignores the reason in favor of the lunacy, for madness is more dramatic than politics and philosophy. Hence, like the Roman party-goers, the French crowds are nourished on frenzy, wine, and blood. The passion that we witnessed during the storming of the Bastille has been ritualized into the actual dance of a Bacchanal. Nothing is more nourishing for a mob than a spell of dancing; hence the French people dance almost every day. In many ways the dance serves the same purpose as knitting, "a something, once innocent, delivered over to all devilry—a healthy pastime changed into a means of angering the blood." As they gnash their teeth, they forget themselves, and five hundred individual human beings become "five hundred demons" who share one purpose, one passion. They are wolves, vampires, monsters. And yet, like most demonic and animal mobs, the individuals who comprise this dance are "good by nature"; it is only when they are together that they exert this perverse power. Indeed, one might think that Dickens has taken the Bacchanalian parallels a little too far. During one dance, for example, the crowds actually see "some ghastly apparition of a dance-figure gone raving mad arise among them,"—an explicit reference to the sightings of the wine-god during the original Roman events.

In their vitality, the French may be the most "Dickensian" characters in *A Tale of Two Cities*. It takes more than one reading to fully appreciate how sympathetic Dickens is to his French mobs. True, they are bloodthirsty, but they are also capable of fantastic sweetness. It is in the French, not the English, that Dickens finds the contradictions suggested in the book's beginning. We have said in the beginning that this is a bipolar book; if we keep this in mind, the French are its schizophrenic stars. Compare Charles Darnay's trial at the Old Bailey to his trial in Paris. The Old Bailey crowd exhibits bloodlust—that is undeniable—but a bloodlust bred from the rather mercantile desire of an audience who has paid good money to see a show. Hence the chapter title "A Disappointment" when Charles is released; for the English crowd feels cheated out of their ha'penny's-worth of drama, and Charles, the acquitted prisoner, makes his way home in semi-disgrace. The French, on the other hand, greet released prisoners with tears of joy. Granted, they are equally ecstatic when someone is condemned; but give them an opportunity to feel, and they will take it.

The crowds retire with empty bellies, but they have been sated with blood. The close of Chapter 22 demonstrates Dickens's genius, and also his compassion in depicting the revolutionary hordes. Full and happy at last, they play with their children, raise a glass of thin wine, and sleep deeply. Just as they are capable of annihilation, so they are capable of tenderness—indeed, the destruction that they wreak only nourishes their capacity to love. In many ways they are more attractive than their pallid English counterparts. Given as they are to feeling, the French are simply more generous.

Another three years pass. In **Chapter 23** and **Chapter 24**, Tellson's Bank, feeding as it does on fear and death, is doing splendid business with the displaced French aristocracy. Mr. Lorry departs for Paris. So does Charles Darnay. His family château has been burned during the revolution, and the faithful family servant, Gabelle, has been imprisoned. Perhaps he is driven by the disparaging comments of Mr. Stryver; Gabelle's letter is addressed to the present Marquis St. Evrémonde, a name that Darnay abandoned long ago but, presumably, disclosed to Dr. Manette on his wedding day. Stryver unknowingly insults Darnay by calling the present marquis a coward, and Darnay sets out to save Gabelle; in doing so, he embarks on the journey to France that Defarge, years ago, hoped he would never undertake.

BOOK III: THE TRACK OF A STORM

Even those who have never read *A Tale of Two Cities* are familiar with Darnay's voyage, or at least its results. He returns to France to save his old servant, and he is arrested; Lucie and her father follow him to Paris. Miss Pross, Mr. Lorry, and little Lucie, Lucie's daughter, keep them company for the next year and a half. Darnay is tried in France twice; the first time he is acquitted, and the second he is sentenced to death. On the eve of Darnay's execution, the lookalike Sidney Carton takes his place in the prison cell. Charles, Lucie, Dr. Manette, and the child escape; Miss Pross shoots the sinister Madame Defarge, and Carton is executed nobly in Darnay's stead.

For much of their Paris adventures (**Chapters 1–6**), Dr. Manette proves crucial. As a former prisoner of the Bastille, and a hardworking doctor, he is immensely popular, and it is his testimony that first saves Darnay from the guillotine. At the very mention of the doctor's name, "[t]ears immediately [roll] down several ferocious countenances which had been glaring at the prisoner before, as if with impatience to pluck him out into the streets and kill him."

The bloodshed in revolutionary France may seem only about revenge, but somewhere behind that is hope. Dr. Manette feels the vitality of the revolutionary spirit; when he crosses the Channel to rescue his son-in-law, he comes alive in a way that we have not seen. He never really belonged in England. In London, he only had his family, and was hopeless without them. He was still a man half-dead, a man whose life "was stopped like a clock," who cowered from the past and hid from the present in his Soho sanctuary. The Dr. Manette of England was a weakling who fell back into his old madness when his daughter left him for her honeymoon. France, however, makes Dr. Manette strong. By returning to this country, he confronts his past; indeed, he rather trumpets his status as a former prisoner of the Bastille. The key to Dr. Manette's strength lies not, as Mr. Lorry thought, in repressing his demons, but grappling with them and using them to his advantage. By **Chapter 4** he has become the man he was before his imprisonment. In fact it is Mr. Lorry who first notices the change: "[T]he calm strong look of the man whose life…[is] set going again with an energy which had lain dormant during the cessation of its usefulness."

This new, vigorous Dr. Manette *likes* being among his people, because they make him feel, to use Lorry's word, *useful*. As much as he protects his daughter Lucie from horrors, he derives enjoyment from his daily routine, chatting with prison guards, negotiating the screaming crowds. He works tirelessly, among the rich and the poor, the imprisoned and the free. He feeds on their love. For, above all, Manette has re-realized himself as a great doctor. Great doctors are like gods, for they alone have the power to restore life. Surely, there is nothing more humiliating for a once-successful doctor to not only have that talent taken away from him, but to also have the life restored to him by others. Lucie provided Dr. Manette with his first resurrection, but it was a half-baked rescue. Back in Paris, Dr. Manette does something much more potent—he resurrects himself.

In doing so, he has become the real man of the household. He is the breadwinner and the problem solver, and while in England he was helpless without his friends and family, in France, they are helpless without him. It cannot be said that this thrill of power is not without its dark overtones. He will *save* Lucie, and he will *save* her husband—and his motives are not entirely unselfish. For in *saving* his daughter and Charles, he repays a debt, and proves his potency to boot. In *saving* Charles also, he replaces his son-in-law as the unquestionable authority of their household; everyone, in future, will respect and defer to him. Manette is a full man, flawed and passionate. Many critics have noted the sexual feelings he harbors for his daughter—the reluctance with which he views her marriage, and the way he rests his head upon her lap. In many ways, Manette resembles Dickens, for though Carton may be the author's obvious doppelgänger, there are reflections of him elsewhere. Dickens finds identification with Charles Darnay, whose name is so similar to his own, as the romantic rebel who is always on trial. Manette also has much in common with his creator, both as a father and as a man who thrives on the adoration of others. Leonard Manheim, in his essay "A Tale of Two Characters," points out that Manette at the beginning of the novel is forty-five, the exact age of Dickens when he wrote the novel. Like Manette, Dickens cannot live by simply supporting those he loves, he is driven by the desire to *save*.

There is something vampiric about Dr. Manette's re-found strength. Lucie is now rapidly fading, and so is her husband. Charles, most interestingly, finds himself slipping into the mentality that once possessed Dr. Manette when he was in prison. "Now I am left," he thinks as the door locks behind him at the start of Book III, "as if I were dead." Just as Dr. Manette made shoes, so Charles paces up and down his cell, and recites mechanically the proportions of his room. Perhaps more eerily, he thinks he can hear the crowd murmuring "He made shoes, he made shoes, he made shoes." It is exactly what Jerry Cruncher means when he says that "[t]here are two sides." One cannot live unless another dies; and one cannot grow powerful unless another weakens. "As my beloved child," Manette tells Mr. Lorry, "was helpful in restoring me to myself, I will be helpful now in restoring the dearest part of herself to her!" There may be something satisfying for him in the role reversal. Gentle Mr. Lorry, who observes the "new sustaining pride" and the Doctor's "new exalted air," might agree.

But Manette's triumph in Darnay's first trial is short-lived, a mere three paragraphs in the text. Less than two hours after his release, Darnay is arrested again and made to stand trial the next day. In **Chapters 7 to 13** unfold the increasingly desperate events that drive the book to its fatal conclusion. Though Madame Defarge is responsible for Charles's arrest, she cannot claim responsibility for sending him to the guillotine. For the second trial, the most damning witness—in a supreme ironic twist—is Dr. Manette himself.

Manette's testimony is in the form of a document that he wrote—in his own blood—when he was a prisoner in the Bastille some thirty years ago. The document, which Defarge retrieved from Manette's old cell during the storming of the

Bastille, answers many of the questions raised in Book II. It explains why Dr. Manette flinched at Darnay's tale of the Tower prisoner, for Manette himself had done the same thing, by immuring this confession in his cell wall. It explains why the Evrémondes are so hated. Above all, the document reveals why Darnay's identity as an Evrémonde drove the doctor insane on his daughter's wedding day.

Its melodramatic contents can be summarized as follows. As a young man, the Dr. Manette was called by the Marquis St. Evrémonde, Charles's uncle, for medical assistance. The patient in question was a peasant woman who had been brutally raped. There was another patient, the woman's brother, who had been stabbed while attempting to avenge his sister's honor. The peasant woman, it turned out, had not only a brother, but also a husband, a father, and a sister, when she had caught the fancy of the Marquis's twin brother, Darnay's father. The Marquis and his brother had tortured and killed her husband and father before taking her hostage and forcing her to submit to their will. Both the woman and her brother died. The doctor was imprisoned when he attempted to communicate the situation to the authorities. He ended the letter cursing the Evrémonde family: "And them and their descendants, to the last of their race, I, Alexandre Manette...denounce to the times when all these things shall be answered for. I denounce them to Heaven and to earth."

It is significant that that crime that has created Madame Defarge is a crime against the feminine, the noble raping the poor. La France—with all her extremes—is portrayed in revolutionary terms as a woman. So is *la Guillotine*, with its mercilessly indiscriminate disposal of life. And *la Révolution* itself has been effigized countless times as a woman in robes, bearing a sword. Men may have weapons, but it is the women who are ruthless. Men have passions, but they fluctuate; women are driven by a motive that does not waver. Here we have the familiar dichotomy of birth and death. Only those who have the power to bring life into the world have the power to take it away. And Madame Defarge, who controls these women, is passion at its purest. Within the novel she is *la Revolution*, as well as its creator. Furthermore, she is beautiful, sensuality incarnate. Her attraction is addictive. The other characters all are linked by "an instinctive recognition...of [her] qualities." Mr. Lorry recognizes Madame Defarge, and so do Dr. Manette, Lucie, and most memorably Miss Pross in Chapter 14, when Madame Defarge is finally killed. Madame Defarge's identity transcends explanation. As Madame enters with a pistol and knife demanding Lucie's whereabouts in French, Miss Pross understands her intentions without understanding a word.

Dickens himself is attracted to Madame Defarge, certainly more than he is to Lucie. Consider the way he describes her. "Of a strong and fearless character, of a shrewd sense and readiness, of great determination, of that kind of beauty which...impart[s] to its possessor firmness and animosity." Dickens has never been more physical with his characters. He dwells on Madame's brown legs, her "rich" dark hair, the way her dress models her breasts. Even Madame's demise is sexy. She and Miss Pross struggle bosom to bosom, before Miss Pross finds the pistol concealed next to Madame's skin and she shoots her. Certain critics have supposed that Dickens modeled Lucie on his new mistress Ellen Ternan; this is improbable, considering that Ternan was a fierce, sometimes cold woman who had lived a hard life. Ternan—about whom little is known—has been likened to Estella from *Great Expectations*, Lizzie Hexham from *Our Mutual Friend*, and Helena Landless of *The Mystery of Edwin Drood*. All three are *femmes fatales*—at once erotic and cold. The physical resemblance between the Helena Landless, arguably the sexiest of those three, and Madame Defarge is particularly notable. They are both tall, dark, and rosy-complexioned, and they both favor the color red. Though Ternan, who was fair-haired and small, probably served as the physical model for Lucie, her spirit much more resides in Madame Defarge.

Madame Defarge is Lucie's opposite and far more seductive; she is to Lucie's character what Carton is to Darnay's. There is a marvelously funny moment at the start of Book III when

Lucie pleads to Madame Defarge for her husband's life. "O sister-woman, think of me," she begs, "As a wife and mother!" Here we have two women, diametrically opposed—one blonde, the other dark, one ethereal, the other voluptuous. That spiritual Lucie should be the only one who has actually experienced childbirth is sublimely ironic. But Lucie is the mother of one little girl. Madame Defarge, apparently barren, is the mother of the new France. Her children are multitudes.

However, the passion that first created Madame Defarge was human in origin. Dickens's least compromising villain turns out to be the most justified; her entire family was slaughtered. To demand the extermination of the family who exterminated one's own does not, in this light, seem all that bad. Other Dickensian heroes, like Nicholas Nickleby, seek revenge for much, much less. Thus Madame Defarge, who seems the most constant of characters, is also a person resurrected. Thirty years ago, a little peasant girl disappeared, and she was recreated as Madame Defarge. This brings us back to why Madame can be characterized as a vampire. Her identity is forged in death; she has the pitilessness of an immortal and a "tigress." Her demonic determination, however, originated from the horror of a little girl whose family has been taken away in the most brutal fashion possible. As a vampire, Madame Defarge is more glorious and vital than the human beings whom she controls. Years pass, and she does not get older. She is still someone who walks with the "freedom of a woman who had habitually walked in her girlhood, barefoot and barelegged, on the brown sea sand." Lucie doesn't get older either, but that is because she is practically ether; Madame Defarge doesn't get older because she renews herself through blood, lust, and desire.

In England, Darnay has shed the Evrémonde name and taken one based on his mother's family, the "good side." In France, however, he is forced to reassume the name of his family once again—and with the death of his uncle he became the current marquis. This also makes Lucie and her daughter Evrémondes. In denouncing the Evrémondes and their descendants, then, Manette has condemned his son-in-law, his daughter, and his granddaughter.

And with Darnay's second trial (**Chapter 12**) ends Dr. Manette's newfound vitality. He suffers another relapse, different and more severe than his experience on Lucie's wedding day. At the conclusion of Charles's first trial, Manette really believes that he has triumphed and restored not only Charles but his daughter as well. He does not falter when Charles is first re-arrested, for he still believes that there is hope. But when the trial reveals that it is he who is the most damning witness against Charles, his world falls apart. For he has failed as a man, as a father, but most of all, as a doctor. He whose newfound pride was wrapped in his talent for giving life now realizes that he has been instrumental in taking that life away. It is too much for him, and he reverts to his shoemaker ways. But Mr. Lorry has burned the bench and tools, perhaps not the wisest of decisions. It proves to be the doctor's absolute extinction. Now he is a nameless shoemaker without that mechanical occupation that once kept him alive; in short, he is now more dead than dead. For the rest of the novel, Dr. Manette is reduced to a mumbling trance. He cannot even stand, let alone walk, and must be carried like the corpse that he has become.

Manette has no more heroism to offer. Fortunately, Sidney Carton has arrived from London. Since Carton was a student in Paris and has a fluent command of French—so unlike Mr. Lorry and Miss Pross, who are helpless in this foreign land—he is able to spy as he pleases. It comes in handy that evening after Charles's conviction, as Carton eavesdrops on the Defarges (Chapter 12). Now we learn why Madame Defarge despises the Evrémonde family: she is the sole survivor of the horrific events described in Manette's letter. She is the younger sister of the peasant woman, whom her brother hid in Paris where the Evrémondes could not get her. Eventually she married Defarge, the former servant to Dr. Manette, and dedicated the rest of her life to doing to the Evrémonde family exactly what it had done to her own. Her vendetta against all Evrémondes is something that Dr. Manette might have applauded thirty years ago; but the only Evrémondes left are Charles, Lucie, and their daughter.

While in Paris Carton also identifies John Barsad, former spy for the Crown, who testified against Charles at the Old Bailey, and who is now living as a Frenchman. Miss Pross identifies him also as her long-lost brother Solomon, who abandoned her in England years ago.

The plot at this point becomes complex with assumed identities. Madame Defarge was a country peasant girl whose family was slain by Charles's father and uncle. John Barsad was Miss Pross's brother, a spy for the English courts who now works as a spy for the French tribunal. Barsad's ally is Roger Cly, who also testified against Charles in England, whose funeral we witnessed, and who has since re-emerged from the grave, also French, like John Barsad. The person who identifies Cly beyond a doubt is Jerry Cruncher; apparently, when Cruncher opened Cly's grave back in Book II, he found nothing but an empty coffin.

In order to understand how Carton is able to manipulate Barsad and Cly, we need to understand the historical context. During this period, England and France's relations were shaky at best, worsened only by England's allegiance to the French crown. England's grievances against the French Republic were various, including the fact that some important French revolutionaries (including the Marquis de Lafayette) had contributed to England's loss of its American colonies just two decades before. This is why Darnay was put on trial at the Old Bailey: back in 1780 he had harbored Revolutionary sympathies. His comment that "perhaps George Washington might gain almost as great a name in history as George the Third" was potentially treasonous. In 1780 John Barsad and Roger Cly were British spies; after Darnay's trial, they went to France to continue to keep an eye on subversive French activities. (It is as a British spy that Barsad introduces himself to Madame Defarge in Book II.) Now, during the Revolution, Barsad and Cly have re-invented themselves as French Republicans, and Carton's knowledge of Barsad and Cly's former activities puts them into a bind; if he exposes them, they will be sent to the guillotine. Thus Carton secures their aid, which is helpful because both work closely with the French tribunal and have access to prisons and prisoners. Carton has everything he needs to change places with Darnay and secure a safe escape for the Manette family.

Like our main characters, Roger Cly and John Barsad can navigate fluently through both London and Paris, and belong to neither one nationality nor the other. Carton, Cly, and Barsad speak French so fluently they are indistinguishable from Frenchmen; Darnay and Lucie are French citizens who have been completely acclimated to English life. In contrast, the rest of the characters, on the other hand, are native to the extreme. The Defarges are Gallic sensuality incarnate, their gang so melodramatic that even Jacques Five, their road-mender, has the hammed-up delivery of a stereotypical French *comédien*. Mr. Lorry, Miss Pross, and Jerry Cruncher are so set in their British ways that, when they travel, they take their country with them. A year and a half passes, in which Pross, Lorry, and Jerry comb the Parisian streets without picking up the customs, or in the case of Pross and Jerry, a syllable of the language.

Being in France only enhances their Britishness, which spreads throughout their environment. Mr. Lorry is the best example of this. He establishes the Paris branch of Tellson's in an unlikely place: a florid, over-decorated hothouse formerly belonging to the same Monseigneur who required four servants to serve him his morning chocolate. Now that Monseigneur has fled, its courtyard houses the grindstone upon which good citizens whet their blood-stained weapons. None of this fazes Mr. Lorry, who effectively turns it into his little bit of efficient London, where everything has its "time and place."

Englishness is in many ways the reason for the redemption of Jerry Cruncher, who is not quite a clean man. His life so far has involved digging up bodies and chatting up wealthy widows. In France, however, his nationality makes him a hero; he is a comfort to the Manette family and instrumental in their escape. He resembles John Barsad and Roger Cly; all are streetwise personalities who skirt the law for the purposes of financial gain. But Barsad and Cly have accomplished this by relinquishing their identities, and, most importantly, their country. Jerry Cruncher, on the other hand, remains true to Jerry Cruncher—with all the British Cruncher quirks—which makes him the truest, if most unconscious, patriot of all. Best, he remains true to himself even at the risk of embarrassment. Jerry does not repent because he does not have to; his morality is due to the fact that he is solid and consistent as the finest British stone. When Lorry realizes that Cruncher has been digging up bodies for a living and asks him about it, Cruncher scratches his head and replies he is an "agicultooral character."

Two Cities is a story of swapped identities and resurrection; all the main characters experience spiritual death and come back as someone else. Even all-too-English Lorry and Pross undergo rebirth of sorts. Lorry at the beginning is one of the bank's "old men" who have been interred until the life has been sucked out of them. His life is restored with his acquaintance with the Manette family. Pross, at the very end, has a horrific experience that makes her lose her hearing. It is ironic, then, that the only character who is *not* resurrected in the entire novel is Cruncher, the "Resurrection-Man" himself. Cruncher is the most Dickensian of characters in this non-Dickensian story, a man driven into his dubious trade. When swearing off his old ways to Mr. Lorry, he also shows himself to be a family man:

> [L]et that there boy keep his father's place, and take care of his mother; don't blow upon that boy's father—do not do it, sir—and let that father go into the line of the reg'lar diggin', and make amends for what he would have undug—if it wos so—by diggin' of 'em in with a will, and with conwictions respectin' the futur' keepin' of 'em safe.

No matter how much he has mistreated them, his family is foremost. He will make amends, but it is for the sake of his son and wife rather than for his own. Indeed, he is the embodiment of Dickens's faith in the common Englishman— a man who has behaved badly, but only to save himself and his family from starvation. And it is Cruncher, in the end, whom Dickens entrusts to point out the book's core truth. In his words,

> There'd be two sides to it. There might be medical doctors at the present hour, a picking up their guineas where a honest tradesman don't pick up his fardens—fardens! no, nor yet his half fardens—half fardens! no, nor yet his quarter—a banking away like smoke at Tellson's, and a cocking their medical eyes at that tradesman on the sly....

Men like Cruncher cannot be as noble as Mr. Lorry because they simply cannot afford it. And yet what cushions Mr. Lorry's pocketbook is exactly what feeds Cruncher. Without men like him, a bank like Tellson's could not exist. Both are sustained by death. Thus it is hypocritical for Lorry to criticize Cruncher. One cannot, in Cruncher's words, "sarse the goose and not the gander."

Lorry and Cruncher both are in the business of resurrecting, and this is a major theme of the book. Almost everyone in *A Tale of Two Cities* is resurrected, usually with a new identity. Solomon Pross becomes John Barsad, who then becomes a French Republican. His colleague Roger Cly goes through an actual funeral, only to be resurrected as another Frenchman. The future Marquis St. Evrémonde leaves France and comes back to life as Charles Darnay, only to have to re-assume his real name in a Parisian prison. Dr. Manette dies a number of times—the first time in the Bastille—and turns into a shoemaker by the name of one hundred and five, North Tower, in order to survive. Lucie Manette rebirths herself into a woman when she becomes Lucie Darnay. But when she ceases to be a Manette, she also cedes her power to revivify her father. In France she is name-confused, and hence weak—she is now neither Manette, Darnay nor Evrémonde and so she forgets herself. Mr. Lorry may not have given up his name, but he died when he joined Tellson's Bank, with its old-man minions who have been ripened in its environs. He leaps back into life only after meeting the Manettes. In perhaps the most chilling switch, Miss Pross loses her hearing after shooting Madame Defarge. As the scene that follows with Jerry Cruncher indicates, Miss Pross loses her usefulness. We do not know what she will become—but as usefulness is intrinsically linked to Miss Pross' identity, we might think that she is headed down the same road as Dr. Manette.

Meanwhile, the French change names and identities all the time. The road-mender of Book II becomes a wood-sawyer. Everywhere in the new republic, streets and shops switch their titles. Even the aristocrats re-birth themselves; the lords change clothes with their chefs in order to sneak over the border. But the most resurrections are done among the common people themselves. Being blessed with a new name is an honor. Madame Defarge's right-hand woman gets the privilege to be a hell-pot the moment she is dubbed the Vengeance. All of Defarge's men take his name Jacques and hence become duplicates of their boss. Moreover, Jacques is not Monsieur Defarge's original name, in Book II, Chapter 16, we learn that his name is actually Ernest. Ernest was a good servant to Doctor Manette. Ernest re-baptizes himself Jacques in order to become the man who has the courage to lead a revolution.

Of course, no one benefits from the re-baptizing and resurrection more than Sidney Carton himself. In Paris, Sidney switches identities well, better even than John Barsad and Roger Cly. "You speak like a Frenchman," Jacques Five tells him. "Ah!" Jacques Five replies when Sidney tells him that he is in fact English, "Perfect Frenchman." Before Sidney comes into himself, he can slip in and out unnoticed. He is unlike Barsad, for Barsad has an unforgettable face. The resemblance he shares with Darnay was discussed at the Old Bailey trial, but it goes further—in his self-effacement, Sidney Carton looks like everyone and no one.

Carton is able to move about as he does because he is not a man, but a walking ghost, a shadow. As a young man, Sidney lost himself. However, the circumstances under which he did so are unclear. After all, Sidney is well-educated, even spending time in France, where Stryver was his cohort and not his employer. "Long ago," Dickens explains, "when he had been famous among his competitors as a youth of great promise, he had followed his father to the grave." Hence, his untimely "death," as he calls it, intersected with that of his father. In order to retrieve himself, therefore, Sidney must revisit literally the moment when his father was interred—and bring back to life the part of himself that lies buried there. Resurrect the father, and we resurrect the son. It is not exactly the subtlest of moments—Sidney walks through the streets of Paris repeating to himself the same words he heard the priest recite at his father's graveside: "I am the resurrection and the life, saith the Lord." In order to bring his father back to life, Carton must believe that his father has never died at all. In short, he has to rediscover his own Christian faith and believe that anyone "who liveth and believeth" in that God "shall never die." Everyone in this novel resurrects, but that the resurrections of the morally good English and morally corrupt French are different, Dickens makes abundantly clear. The French resurrect their people through vampire-pagan-voodoo-magic; the English resurrect theirs through God. Dickens emphasizes this; in Sidney Carton's case, his resurrection is synonymous with his re-baptism. He asks Mr. Lorry, "Does your childhood seem far off?" Both Lorry and Carton had forgotten their boyhood for most of their lives, but now, faced with impending death, they remember sitting on their mother's laps. Death makes them young again. Mr. Lorry replies, "For, as I draw closer and closer to the end, I travel in the circle, nearer and nearer to the beginning." In Mr. Lorry's case, it is old age that brings the memories back. In Carton's, it is his impending sacrifice. So Carton, as he prepares himself for his final intercourse with the guillotine, is more alive than he has ever been. For these Christians, the most beautiful resurrection is a death that is pure, actual, and simple.

But before Sidney can re-birth himself as the noble Sidney Carton that never was, he has to assume another identity—that of Charles Darnay. Carton and Darnay not only share one face, but they share the same two languages also, for both men are equally expert in English and French. Charles Darnay's life is also fresh for the taking. Since his return to France, Charles

Darnay has ceased to exist. He is Charles Evrémonde, prisoner and traitor; on top of that he is half the man he once was, sleepwalking through the same death-like trance as Dr. Manette before him. It must be gratifying for Carton to rearrange his hair and tidy up his clothes (as he does in Chapter 12) and have it remarked by someone no less sharp than Madame Defarge that he and Darnay are "a good deal like!" For a few moments, Sidney Carton can assume the likeness of the man whose life and wife he has always coveted. I would also like to point out that Charles is never allowed to become Charles Darnay again. His departure from France is humiliating. Carton drugs him and then has him carried out of the prison cell. He never regains consciousness, even when the Manettes are fleeing from Paris. In fact, the last name that Charles bears before he crosses the French border is that of "Sidney Carton, Advocate"—the name of the man who Charles has looked down on. Carton offers his physical life to Charles, but in return, Charles relinquishes his life as a husband, father, and man.

Sidney Carton before his execution is allowed to reassume the identity of Sidney Carton once again. A little laundry girl, also condemned, is the first to recognize him as a different man. In his last moments traveling to the guillotine, Carton must hide his face. It is the only time he can be recognized as himself. "It is a far, far better thing that I do than I have ever done," he famously breathes as he ascends to his death. But what Carton accomplishes goes beyond "a far, far better thing." He transforms himself into a far, far better man—a better man than anyone in the book, including Dr. Manette and Charles Darnay. Even more satisfying, this better man is no one but Sidney Carton. Other men empower themselves by taking on a different name; Sidney Carton, on the other hand, reasserts his own. He does not have to take another name to be the hero, because the hero has been in him all along.

All in all, things end on a happy note. In the words of John Gross, "*A Tale of Two Cities* ends fairly cheerfully with its hero getting killed." Sidney Carton ascends to the guillotine a true hero at last. He even—like all romantic heroes—gets his wedding scene. The little seamstress takes his hand in the cart, and as they approach the instrument that will take both their lives, it becomes an altar. "...these two children of the Universal Mother...have come together on the dark highway, to repair home together, and to rest in her bosom." There is no vow more binding than that of shared death. The seamstress herself is a shadow of Lucie, and indeed, of all the women who have graced this story, for in sewing, she represents both the golden thread and the knitted yarn of fate. "She kisses his lips, he kisses hers, they solemnly bless each other." Thus closes the circle that Dickens himself has created. Life and death are one.

Nevertheless, there are still some loose threads. The end is happy because Dickens has willed it so. In this final, optimistic scene, Dickens deliberately ignores the trauma that he has put us through. Dickens cheers us with Carton's final soliloquy, where, like the martyrs before him, Carton prophesies a sunny future for the people for whom he has sacrificed his life. "I see Her with a child upon her bosom, who bears my name. I see her father, aged and bent, but otherwise restored." Lucie has a son whom she names Sidney. Paris is resurrected. The Manette/Darnay family is happy and content.

In so many ways, Carton's vision is a sham, and Dickens himself knows it. In other novels, he allows his endings to act themselves out. By summarizing his happy ending in Sidney's prophecy, Dickens hints that he cannot believe in it himself. Things have been broken that cannot be mended. Compare Carton's words to the last glimpse of the Manette family as they leave France: Manette leaves "helpless, inarticulately murmuring," and Charles Darnay lies in the cart in a "swoon." There is no way that these people can recover. Miss Pross is deaf, from the experience of taking a human life. Charles Darnay, in being rescued, is emasculated. Moreover, Doctor Manette is mad, from that particular anguish that one can only achieve by causing it upon oneself. Dickens cannot bring himself to describe the "prosperous and happy" life that Sidney Carton foretells for them, because it is too impossible. Manette cannot again become the doctor that he proved himself to be in Paris, tirelessly saving lives. Darnay, in cowering from his death, can never be the man whom Lucie can love and respect. Carton may have sacrificed himself for this family, but the grace that he offers is temporary. It is the vampiric image again: By taking his own life, Carton has given life to others, but it is only a half-existence. Carton will be immortal; those for whom he has died will languish in his image. Moreover, by dying, he has also reclaimed his own life in full. The people to whom he literally donates his blood will not live, but merely survive in twilight.

Works Cited

Ackroyd, Peter. *Dickens*. New York: HarperPerennial, 1992.

Barzun, Jacques. *From Dawn to Decadence: 500 Years of Western Cultural Life: 1500 to the Present*. New York: HarperCollins, 2000.

Chesterton, G.K. *Charles Dickens*. London: Burns and Oates, 1975.

Collins, Phillip. *Dickens and Crime*. New York: St. Martin's Press, 1962.

Ford, George H., and Lauriat Lane Jr., eds. *The Dickens Critics*. Ithaca: Cornell University Press, 1961.

Goldberg, Michael K. *Carlyle and Dickens*. Athens: University of Georgia Press, 1972.

Schama, Simon. *Citizens: A Chronicle of the French Revolution*. New York: Knopf, 1989.

Critical Views

CATES BALDRIDGE ON INDIVIDUALISM IN THE NOVEL

It is important to remember, however, that up until the time when the novel's main characters are all assembled in Revolutionary Paris, Sydney is at best a radically defective Doppelgänger of Charles. In fact, early on, the former's "doublings" of the latter serve merely to emphasize the distance which separates them. When first juxtaposed at the trial, they appear "so like each other in feature, so unlike each other in manner" (p. 108), and soon afterwards Carton admits that he resents a mirror-image who only serves to remind him "what [he has] fallen away from" (p. 116). In England, Darnay appears as a close-dangling but ultimately frustrating possibility, his physical resemblance suggesting that closer communion between men *should* be possible, the pair's mutual unintelligibility underscoring how difficult it is, under prevailing circumstances, to achieve. It is only later in Paris, when Sydney determines to sacrifice himself for Darnay and Lucy, that the doublings become nearly perfect. Indeed, "doubling" is too pallid a word to describe adequately what goes on, for such a term still implies two separate identities, two discrete selves, whereas what actually occurs is more properly described as a veritable *merging* of two individuals into one.

The central irony which emerges from Carton's successful commingling with Darnay in prison is that Sydney's "cure" is effected in the shadow of the novel's explicit condemnation of the very practice which heals him, for while he participates in a process whereby one man is able to transcend the suffocating barriers of the bourgeois self, the Revolution's insistence that the same *is* to be done for *all* men meets with nothing but *scorn*. And here one can anticipate an objection: the obvious fact that Sydney and the Jacquerie see the annihilation of the conventional barriers between individuals as the means to ends which are diametrically opposed does not weaken this irony to the extent that one might initially suppose. Yes, Carton abandons his personal claims for the protection of bourgeois domesticity (one might even say for the Victorian hearth, since Sydney's figurative descendents are to recount his story for generations) while the Paris Tribunal demands that the individual subsume himself into the policy in order to speed the flourishing of, as the narrator puts it, the Republic One and Indivisible of Liberty, Equality, Fraternity, or Death. But my point is that the former cause rests upon the foundation stone of bourgeois individualism while the latter is committed to its destruction, and that Carton can only ensure the safety of Liberal society (in the form of the Darnays, Manette, Lorry, and Pross) by temporarily violating one of its fundamental tenets. To put it another way, Carton can only make the world safe for discrete subjects by temporarily ceasing to be one himself and thereby blocking the plans of a regime bent on abolishing the entire concept of the discrete subject forevermore.

Before taking up Sydney's story again, though, we must once more look briefly at the novel's orthodox denigration of Revolutionary practices. As Darnay's second trial gets underway, the Tribunal's attack upon "selfish" bourgeois individualism is in full swing. When Manette protests that he would never violate his domestic circle by denouncing his son-in-law to officers of the state-on account of his "daughter, and those dear to hear" being "far dearer to [him] than [his] life"— the President reminds him that his priorities are dangerously counter-revolutionary:

> "Citizen Manette, be tranquil. To fail in submission to the authority of the Tribunal would be to put yourself out of Law. As to what is dearer to you than life, nothing can be so dear to a good citizen as the Republic."

> Loud acclamations hailed this rebuke. The President rang his bell, and with warmth resumed.

> "If the Republic should demand of you the sacrifice of your child herself, you would have no duty but to sacrifice

her. Listen to what is to follow. In the meantime, be silent!"

(p.346)

Later, when Manette's own testament has been read and the inevitable verdict of "guilty" delivered, the narrator's account is strangely divided between horror and understanding. With biting irony, he recounts how the President suggests "that the good physician of the Republic would deserve better still of the Republic by rooting out an obnoxious family of Aristocrats, and would doubtless feel a sacred glow and joy in making his daughter a widow and her child and orphan" (p.362). One can clearly hear in this passage the revulsion of a good Victorian—and yet, when explaining the scene as a whole, he calmly and fair-mindedly informs us that "one of the frenzied aspirations of the populace was, for imitations of the questionable public virtues of antiquity, and for sacrifices and self-immolations on the people's altar" (p. 362). For now, we will leave the book's conventional depiction of the Revolution with the surprising mildness of the phrase "questionable public virtues" still resonating and turn once more to Carton.

As Sydney takes his famous midnight walk the night before the second Parisian trial, his steps are dogged by religious images, and he repeats "I am the resurrection and the life" continually to himself as he wanders. At one point, though, he pauses to sleep, and, in a moment obviously fraught with symbolic meaning, awakes to find an analogue of his life in the motions of the Seine:

> The strong tide, so swift, so deep, and certain, was like a congenial friend, in the morning stillness. He walked by the stream, far from the houses, and in the light and warmth of the sun fell asleep on the bank. When he awoke and was afoot again, he lingered there yet a little longer, and watching an eddy that turned and turned purposeless, until the stream absorbed it, and carried it on to the sea.—"Like me!"

(p.344)

When on considers that Sydney has resolved to sacrifice himself in order to thwart the collectivist wrath of the Revolution, this passage reads curiously indeed, for cutting across the obvious message concerning Carton's lassitude giving way to action, there is the further hint that to do so involves subsuming himself in a larger entity. One could perhaps suggest that he is being "absorbed" into the greater life of humanity at large or into the Christian dispensation were it not for the quite programmatic way in which "tide" and "sea" have been associated throughout *A Tale* with the revolutionary mob. The "strong side, so swift, so deep, and certain" which now appears as Carton's "congenial friend" and into which his life is "absorbed" may not partake of the violence of that which breaks against the Bastille, but the provocative choice of simile cannot help but alert us to a parallel between Sydney's path to personal salvation and the Revolution's recipe for a secular utopia beyond the constraints of bourgeois individualism.

Sir James Fitzjames Stephen on Dickens and Exaggeration

One special piece of grotesqueness introduced by Mr. Dickens into his present tale is very curious. A good deal of the story relates to France, and many of the characters are French. Mr. Dickens accordingly makes them talk a language which, for a few sentences, is amusing enough, but which becomes intolerably tiresome and affected when it is spread over scores of pages. He translates every French word by its exact English equivalent. For example, "Voilà votre passeport" becomes "Behold your passport"—"Je viens de voir," "I come to see" &c. Apart from the bad taste of this, it shows a perfect ignorance of the nature and principles of language. The sort of person who would say in English, "Behold," is not the sort of person who would say in French "Voilà"; and to describe the most terrible event in this misbegotten jargon shows a great want of sensibility to the real requirements of art. If an acquaintance with Latin were made the excuse for a similar display, Mr. Dickens and his disciples would undoubtedly consider such conduct as inexcusable pedantry. To show off familiarity with a modern language is not very different from similar conduct with respect to an ancient one.

The moral tone of the *Tale of Two Cities* is not more wholesome than that of its predecessors, nor does it display any nearer approach to a solid knowledge of the subject matter to which it refers. Mr. Dickens observes in his preface—"It has been one of my hopes to add something to the popular and picturesque means of understanding to the philosophy of Mr. Carlyle's wonderful book." The allusion to Mr. Carlyle confirms the presumption which the book itself raises, that Mr. Dickens happened to have read the History of the French Revolution, and, being on the look-out for a subject, determined off-hand to write a novel about it. Whether he has any other knowledge of the subject than a single reading of Mr. Carlyle's work would supply does not appear, but certainly what he has written shows no more. It is exactly the sort of story which a man would write who had taken down Mr. Carlyle's theory without any sort of inquiry or examination, but with a comfortable conviction that "nothing could be added to its philosophy." The people, says Mr. Dickens, in effect, had been degraded by long and gross misgovernment, and acted like a wild beasts in consequence. There is, no doubt, a great deal of truth in this view of the matter, but it is such very elementary truth that, unless a man had something new to say about it, it is hardly worth mentioning; and Mr. Dickens supports it by specific assertions which, if not absolutely false, are at any rate so selected as to convey an entirely false impression. It is a shameful thing for a popular writer to exaggerate the faults of the French aristocracy in a book which will naturally find its way to readers who know very little of the subject except what he chooses to tell them; but it is impossible not the feel that the melodramatic story which Mr. Dickens tells about the wicked Marquis who violates on of his serfs and murders another, is a grossly unfair representation of the state of society in France in the middle of the eighteenth century. That the French *noblesse* had much to answer for in a thousand ways, is a lamentable truth; but it is by no means true that they could rob, murder, and ravish with impunity. When Count Horn thought proper to try the experiment under the Regency, he a broken on the wheel, notwithstanding his nobility; and the sort of atrocities which Mr. Dickens depicts as characteristic of the eighteenth century were neither safe nor common in the fourteenth.

England as well as France comes in for Mr. Dickens's factors. He takes a sort of pleasure, which appears to us insolent and unbecoming in the extreme, in drawing the attention of his readers exclusively to the bad and weak points in the history and character of their immediate ancestors. The grandfathers of the present generation were, according to him, a sort of savages, or very little better. They were cruel, bigoted, unjust, ill-governed, oppressed, and neglected in every possible way. The childish delight with which Mr. Dickens acts Jack Horner, and says What a good boy am I, in comparison with my benighted ancestors, is thoroughly contemptible. England some ninety years back was not what it is now, but it was a very remarkable country. It was inhabited and passionately loved by some of the greatest men who were then living, an it possessed institutions which, with many imperfections, were by far the best which then existed in the world, and were, amongst other things, the sources from which our present liberties are derived. There certainly were a large number of abuses, but Mr. Dickens is not content with representing them fairly. He grossly exaggerates their evils. It is usually difficult to bring a novelist precisely to book, and Mr. Dickens is especially addicted to the cultivation of a judicious vagueness; but in his present work he affords an opportunity for instituting a comparison between the facts on which he relies and the assertions which he makes on the strength of them.

EDWIN M. EIGNER ON THE CHARACTER OF DARNAY

Readers and critics, until recently, at any rate, have found Dickens' romantic heroes among the least interesting of his characters, and Darnay is certainly no exception in this regard. He has differed from the other heroes who end up with the girls, however, in that, from the beginning, and in spite of the facts that his manners are impeccable and usually calculated not to give offense, he has inspired animosity both from those within the novel and those outside it. If we could forgive the wicked Marquis de St. Evremonde anything, perhaps it would be for what "Albert Hutter, in a brilliant essay, calls, his "murderous impulses towards his brother's child,"[6] for Charles holds himself morally superior to his uncle and openly rejects everything the latter stands for. This is, I believe, the only time in the novel he takes such a tone. Nevertheless, it is understandable, I suppose, that Madame Defarge and the revolutionaries should see Charles, whether mistakenly or not, as their enemy, the symbol of their oppression. Even the Old Bailey crowd in England can perhaps be excused for their disappointment at not getting to see him half-hanged, then taken down and sliced before his own face, then have his insides burnt while he looks on, then have his head chopped off, and then have his body cut into quarters. Maybe there is not anything personal in this. One could not hope, moreover, that Charles would be especially popular with his English romantic rivals. It is to be expected, therefore, that Stryver should "believe there is a contamination in such a scoundrel"[7] and that Carton should simply "hate the fellow."[8] Nor should be surprised at the negative feelings of those millions of readers who have identified with Carton and felt his rejection by Lucie as if it were their own. Even Charles is quick to excuse his father-in-law for condemning him and his descendants "to the last of their race."[9] It's what he's come to expect. Nevertheless, some of the dislike for Darnay goes beyond the explanations provided.

Less than a month after the last chapter of the novel was published, James Fitzjames Stephen wrote to express his contempt for this coward who "thought he had better live by his wits in London than have the responsibility of continuing a landowner in France,"[10] and Lawrence Frank, a recent interpreter, sees Charles as a self-deceiver, who "lives 'unknown in England,' where he is 'no Marquis': unknown to this tenants in France, unknown to his wife, unknown, finally to himself."[11] In the centennial year of Dickens's death, 1970, the French critic Sylvere Monod noted the "unusually unanimous critical feeling against" Darnay, citing the condemnations of John Gross, K.J. Fielding, and Edgar Johnson. He concludes the summary with his own conviction that while Dickens identified Darnay with himself, "lending him his own leaning towards 'The Loadstone Rock'," he did not give Darnay "more than .01 percent" of his own vitality.[12]

Jack Lindsay was, I believe, the first to note this identification of Dickens with Darnay when he pointed out that the latter "has the revealing initials Charles D."[13] Charles's real name, Evremonde, has also been seen as significant, but in an almost opposite way. Robert Alter believes it suggests the character is "a sort of Everman,"[14] and Elliot Gilbert, in a paper delivered at the 1982 Santa Cruz Dickens Conference and printed in the present volume, call the name "a multi-lingual, two-cities pun on 'everyman' or 'all-the-world.'"[15] At another paper delivered at the same conference, Garrett Steward emphasized the sudden grammatical shift into the first person plural in Book the Third, Chapter 13. The reader, as Stewart suggested, is virtually "conscripted" to accompany the drugged Darnay as the coach takes him, Mr. Lorry, Mr. Manette, and the two Lucies away from the danger in Paris.

Perhaps these insights, beginning the Alter's, provides clues to Darnay's unpopularity. If Dickens wants to identify such a character with himself, that is one matter; but if he is going to try to force us to accept such an identification, that is something else again. But why should we object? Charles is good-looking, well-born, well-bred, well-educated, intelligent, fortunate in both life and love. If he does not have Charles Dickens' vitality, he at least has his industry, and if the aristocratic Fitzjames Stephen wants to call schoolteaching "living by one's wits," why should literary critics, who are most of them schoolteachers themselves, want to share the contempt?

I think an answer to this question and also to the question of why Charles is so disliked within the novel may lie in the way this hero regards himself. Darnay's self-contempt is not so Byronically obvious as Carton's, but I suspect it is deeper and more difficult to transcend, at least by his own efforts. Think, for instance, of the meek way he accepts Carton's insolence after the English trial and the modest way he presses his claim to Lucie when he asks for her father not to oppose his courtship.

> I have felt [he says], and do feel even now, that to bring my love—even mine—between you [and Lucie], is to touch your history with something not quite so good as itself.[16]

At the level of the book's religious allegory, he is, of course, Everyman, suffering from original sin. In this regard, Taylor Stoehr has written that "Darnay's guilt appears to be hereditary."[17] Albert Hutter and Lawrence Frank, moreover, in articles previously cited, have both argued convincingly that he is guilty also of a kind of parricide, having imagined or wiled the death of his father's twin brother, the evil Marquis, just hours or perhaps minutes before the latter's murder. But one does not need a Christian or a Freudian interpretation to understand the guilt feelings of a man who was told by his mother when he was two years old that unless he can find and reconcile the needle-in-a-haystack sister of the peasant girl his father had wronged, "atonement would one day be required of him."[18] Moreover, guilt is a specialty of the romantic hero in Dickens' later novels.

Notes

6. "Nation and Generation in *A Tale of Two Cities*," *PMLA*, 93 (1978), 450.

7. *A Tale of Two Cities* (Harmondsworth: Penguin, 1970), Book the Second, Chapter 24, p. 269.

8. Book the Second, Chapter 4, p. 116.

9. Book the Third, Chapter 10, p. 361.

10. "*A Tale of Two Cities*," *Saturday Review*, 17 Dec. 1839, 741

11. "Dickens' *A Tale of Two Cities*: The Poetics of Impasse," *American Imago*, XXXVI (1979), 231.

12. "Dickens's Attitudes in *A Tale of Two Cities*," in *Dickens Centennial Essays*, Ada Nisbet and Blake Nevius, eds. (Berkeley; University of California Press, 1971), p. 177.

13. "*A Tale of Two Cities*," *Life and Letters and The London Mercury*, LXII (1949), 196.

14. "The Demons of History in Dickens' *Tales*" *Novel: A Forum of Fiction*, II (1969), p. 196.

15. P. 259.

16. Book the Second, Chapter 10, p. 163.

17. *Dickens: The Dreamer's Stance* (Ithaca: Cornell University Press, 1965), p. 198.

18. Book the Third, Chapter 10, p. 360.

JOHN GROSS ON CARTON AND DARNAY

A Tale of Two Cities is a tale of two heroes. The theme of the double has such obvious attractions for a writer preoccupied with disguises, rival impulses, and hidden affinities that it is surprising that dickens didn't make more use of it elsewhere. But no one could claim that his handling of the device is very successful here, or that he has managed to range the significant forces of the novel behind Carton and Darnay. Darnay is, so to speak, the accredited representative of Dickens in the novel, the 'normal' hero for whom a happy ending is still possible. It has been noted, interestingly enough, that he shares his creator's initials—and that is pretty well the only interesting thing about him. Otherwise he is a pasteboard character, completely undeveloped. His position as an exile, his struggles as a language-teacher, his admiration for George Washington are so many openings thrown away.

Carton, of course, is a far more striking figure. He belongs to the line of cultivated wastrels who play an increasingly large part in Dickens's novels during the second half of his career, culminating in Eugene Wrayburn; his clearest predecessor, as his name indicates, is the luckless Richard Carstone of *Bleak House*. He has squandered his gifts and drunk away his early promise; his will is broken, but his intellect is unimpaired. In a sense, his opposite is not Darnay at all, but the aggressive

Stryver, who makes a fortune by picking his brains. Yet there is something hollow about his complete resignation to failure: his self-abasement in front of Lucie, for instance. ('I am like one who died young....I know very well that you can have no tenderness for me....') For, stagy a figure though he is, Carton does suggest what Thomas Hardy calls 'fearful unfulfilments'; he still has vitality, and it is hard to believe that he has gone down without a struggle. The total effect is one of energy held unnaturally in check: the bottled-up frustration which Carton represents must spill over somewhere.

Carton's and Darnay's fates are entwined from their first meeting, at the Old Bailey trial. Over the dock there hangs a mirror: 'crowds of the wicked and the wretched had been reflected in it, and had passed from its surface and this earth's together. Haunted in a most ghastly manner that abominable place would have been, if the glass could ever have rendered back its reflections, as the ocean is one day to give up its dead.' (Bk. 11, Ch. 2.) After Darnay's acquittal we leave him with Carton, 'so like each other in feature, so unlike in manner, both reflected in the glass above them.' Reflections, like ghosts, suggest unreality and self-division, and at the end of the same day Carton stares at his own image in the glass and upbraids it: 'Why should you particularly like a man who resembles you? There is nothing in you to like: you know that. Ah, confound you!...Come on, and have it out in plain words! You hate the fellow.' (Bk. II, Ch. 4) In front of the mirror, Carton thinks of changing places with Darnay; at the end of the book, he is to take the other's death upon him. Dickens prepares the ground: when Darnay is in jail, it is Carton who strikes Mr. Lorry as having 'the wasted air of a prisoner', and when he is visited by Carton on the rescue attempt, he thinks at first that he is 'an apparition of his own imaging'. But Dickens is determined to stick by Darnay: a happy ending *must* be possible. As Lorry and his party gallop to safety with the drugged Darnay, there is an abrupt switch to the first person: 'The wind is rushing after us, and the clouds are flying after us, and the moon is plunging after us, and the whole wild night is in pursuit of us; but a far, we are pursued by nothing else.' (Bk. III, Ch. 13) *We* can make our escape, however narrowly; Carton, expelled from our system, must be abandoned to his fate.

But the last work is with Carton—the most famous last work in Dickens, in fact. Those we take a simplified view of Dickens's radicalism, or regard him as one of nature's Marxists, can hardly help regretting that *A Tale of Two Cities* should end as it does. They are bound to feel, with Edgar Johnson, that 'instead of merging, the trust of revolution and the truth of sacrifice are made to appear in conflict'. A highly personal, indeed a unique crisis cuts across public issues and muffles the political message. But this is both to sentimentalize Dickens's view of the revolution, and to miss the point about Carton. The cynical judgment that his sacrifice was trifling, since he had nothing to live for, is somewhat nearer the mark. Drained of the will to live, he is shown in the closing chapters of the book as a man courting death, and embracing it when it comes. 'In seasons of pestilence, some of us will have a secret attraction to the disease—a terrible passing inclination to die of it. And all of us have like wonders hidden in our breasts, only needing circumstances to evoke them.' (Bk. III, Ch. 6) It is Carton rather than Darnay who is 'drawn to the loadstone rock'.[1] On his last walk around Paris, a passage which Shaw cites in the preface to Man and Superman as proof of Dickens's essentially irreligious nature, his thoughts run on religion: 'I am the Resurrection and the Life.' But his impressions are all of death: the day comes coldly, 'looking like the dead face out of the sky' while on the river 'a trading boat, with a sail of the softened colour of a dead leaf, then gilded into his view, floated by him, and died away'. (Bk. III, Ch.9.) His walk recalls an earlier night, when he wandered round London with 'wreaths of dust spinning round and round before the morning blast, as if the desert sand had risen far away and the first spray of it in its advance had begun to overwhelm the city'. (Bk. II, Ch. 5.) Then, with the wilderness bringing home to him a sense of the wasted powers within him, he saw a momentary mirage of what he might have achieved and was reduced to tears; but now that the city has been overwhelmed in earnest, he is past thinking of what might have been. "It is a far, far better thing that I do, than I have ever done'—but the 'better thing' might just as well be committing suicide as laying down his life for Darnay. At any rate, he thinks of himself as going towards rest, not towards resurrection.

Note

1. Darnay, who only comes to life in the face of death, is nevertheless obsessed with the guillotine. He has 'a strange besetting desire to know what to do when the time came, a desire gigantically disproportionate to the few swift moments to which it referred; a wondering that was more like the wondering of some other spirit within his, than his own.' (Bk. III, Ch. 13) Carton's spirit, perhaps; through the exigencies of the plot, Dickens has got the wires crossed.

JOHN B. LAMB ON THE NOVEL AS ASYLUM

The nineteenth-century novel becomes the site for the re-evolution and recovery not only of the characters, but of the reader as well. The novel is the locus of moral therapy, because like the asylum it provides an imaginary substitute for the social and familiar environment. The novel as asylum seeks to re-educate its readers, to re-create correct patterns of thinking and to re-establish appropriate standards of behavior.

In *A Tale of Two Cities*, domestic space is no longer the opposite of the asylum, no longer the private home from which the insane individual is removed and to which he or she must return. It is the asylum, and as such, it is the specific location for the management of political and sexual transgression. It harbors the pathology that is history as its double, containing, controlling, and canceling it. And just as Lucie's home is the site for Carton's transformation, so too the nineteenth-century novel turns readers into what Foucault calls "docile bodies" that may be "subjected, used, transformed, and improved" (*Discipline and Punish* 131). In his engagement with the novel the reader is uprooted from his familiar historical environment—England in the late 1850's, the site of contemporary forces of sexual and political disruption—and relocated in a special environment whose internal economy, the triumph of domestic ideology over revolution, embodies the order whose repeated interiorization is the condition for his successful integration and "return" to the real world. Here, the reader is exposed to the fate of those like Madame Defarge who have failed to interiorize the values that order bourgeois society.

Novel reading, particularly the reading of serialized novels like *A Tale of Two Cities*, mimics the patterns of managed asylum life, redistributing time. It replaces the processive "history" of reading with a monthly exercise, with discrete and yet homogenous experiences of the text's duration and its ideology. The privacy of novel reading isolates the reader from the outside world, from the uncontrollable and contradictory forces of history, which is the place where his disorder is produced, and transplants him into an imaginatively ordered space co-extensive with the domesticity itself. As Linda K. Hughes and Michael Lund suggest, "the virtues that sustain a home and the traits required of serial readers so often coincided" (16). In this ordered therapeutic space, the reader lives in the "lucidity of the law," a law he once more makes his own. In the world of the novel, as in the asylum, moral order is "reduced to its bare bones of law, obligations, and constraints," and the novel functions as the model of an ideal society, "in the sense of being ideally reduced to order" (Castel, *The Regulation of Madness* 75).

The imposition of ideal order by the novel is backed by the relationship of authority between the novelist and the reader. Similar to nineteenth-century psychiatric reformers, dickens attacks the more violent forms of treatment of the insane, symbolized in Dr. Manette's incarceration in the Bastille, while instituting the "invisible" discipline of moral management and the managing function of the asylum of everyday life. *A Tale of Two Cities* is an elaborate case history of the diagnosis, treatment, and cure of the social body infected with the pathology of revolution. Dickens casts himself in the role of the attending physician or benevolent asylum head and his narrator evinces those qualities without which "no man can be personally successful in the moral treatment of the insane":

> A faculty of seeing that which is passing in the minds of men is the first requisite of moral power and discipline, whether in asylums, schools, parishes, or elsewhere. Add to this a firm will, the faculty of self-control, a sympathizing distress at moral pain, a strong desire to remove it, and that biologizing power is elicited, which enables men to domineer for good purposes over the minds of others.
>
> (Bucknill and Tuke 489)

The "power" which allows the novelist to "domineer" for moral purposes over the minds of his readers is clearly taxonomic, an ordering of signs. Like the expert in moral treatment, dickens carefully nominates, codifies, and regulates the behavior of the characters in his novel in his attempt to "declare the truth" about revolution.[8] The novelist, like the asylum physician, is omnipotent, if not completely omniscient: "innermost personality," Dickens admits, is ultimately "inscrutable" (44). His power lies, therefore, not in the knowledge of the sexual or political secrets at the heart of social disorder and individual pathology, but in his control over the signs which confirm that such secretes must and do exist. The novelist is a specialist in the symptomatology of social disorder, and Dickens "seeks the narratable in what which deviates most markedly from normal, in the criminal, the outside-the-law, the unsocialized, and the ungoverned" (Brooks 153). Unable to fathom the root causes of social anomie, he directs attention instead to the signs or symptoms of social unrest, and those signs are simply those which "distinguish pathological behavior from socially regulated modes of conduct" (Castel, *The Regulation of Madness* 97). Such symptoms—like Carton's lassitude or Madame Defarge's malice—signify a preponderance of moral causes, particularly political and sexual transgression, which in turn legitimize moral therapy (here, in the form of domestic ideology) as the only means of treatment capable of eradicating the moral causes of pathology and restoring the insane individual to rationality, to the regulated modes of conduct that constitute the bourgeois, domestic norm. The relationship of the novelist and his reader is, therefore, analogous to that between the doctor and the patient; it is a relationship of authority that binds the novelist to the reader "in the exercise of a power that [lacks] reciprocity" (Castel, *The Regulation of Madness* 75), since it is only the novelist who can order the signs that designate transgressive behavior. Such a relationship suggests that he reader suffers from the disorder of moral insanity, from those "buried" but no less transgressive energies that political events and social conflict, or history generate. The novel interpellates the reader/subject as "free" and responsible for his own actions, as the point of origin of his own transgression and cure. Although readers may aspire to the ideal of characters like Lucie Manette or Jarvis Lorry, the determinate names the novel designates for them are "Thérèse Defarge" or "Sidney Carton." The novel as asylum is a "world constructed in the image of the rationality" (Castel, *The Regulation of Madness* 76) embodied by the novelist, and the novel multiplies his power, since the order of things that triumph in the novel— domesticity and rationality—come to life as a moral order backed by society itself. Thus, the diagnosis and judgment of pathology at the heart of the Victorian novel becomes for the reader a social reality. It is only when he has regained his rational autonomy, has interiorized domestic ideology, that the novel pronounces him cured. It is only when he puts down the novel that the novelist's power is ostensibly canceled.

That power, however, is never really canceled, since the novel and the world "outside" are constructed by the same ideology. The reader's return of the world of lived experience, therefore, merely attests to the "truth" of the novel and the novelist's disciplinary vision. For the discourse of the novel, like moral management, is constructed around a social perception of health, ordered by the same moral symptomatology and symbology, and permeated by the values of the middle class. Domestic ideology, moral management, and the nineteenth-century novel are all forms of authoritarian pedagogy, of a re-educational process that seeks to suppress the focuses of sexual and political revolt and to extinguish them at their source—the revolutionary, "morally insane," subject. But just as *A Tale of Two Cities* betrays a societal anxiety about the forces of history, it also betrays an anxiety about the doctor's or novelist's power to morally manage transgression and cure the pathological. For if revolution and madness are marked by "restlessness," so, too, is writing; and throughout the 1850s, a period of intense personal restlessness for Dickens, he equates that restlessness, and indeed madness, with novel production itself."[9] As Peter Brooks points out, "The plotted novel is a deviance from or transgression of the normal, a state of abnormality and error which alone is 'narratable'" (84-85). The "ferocious excitement" of writing that caused Dickens to run "wildly about and about" a new novel in his own creative carmagnole is a form of imbalance that Dickens appears powerless to cure and Dickens often appears in his letters to be as much writing's victim as its master.

Doctor Manette cannot save Madame Defarge's sister from her madness, from the "high fever of her brain," (331) a "frenzy" so great that he does not even unfasten the bandages that restrain her. Thus, Dickens' novel unconsciously draws a disturbing parallel between the State bonds that the brothers Evremonde use to imprison Defarge's sister and the domestic bonds or "golden threads" that Lucie employs to save Carton and her husband from moral insanity and revolution. Lucie's threads, therefore, are "invisible" ideological counterpart of the Evremondes' more brutal and arbitrary forms of incarceration and disguise the violence at the heart of domestic ideology. Rather than liberating the reader, rather than making him a "free" and autonomous subject, the novel as asylum places him "within a moral element where he will be in debate with himself and his surroundings to constitute for him a milieu where, far from being protected, he will be kept in perpetual anxiety, ceaselessly threatened by Law and Transgression" (Foucault, *Civilization and Madness* 245). The novel, like Tellson's bank, is a place to "mediate on your misspent life," and attests to the truth of the Marquis St. Evremonde's observation, "Repression is the only lasting philosophy" (153).

Notes

8. John Conolly maintains that the business of the asylum physician is "to declare the truth." *On Some of the Forms of Insanity*, p. 85.

9. Writing to Forster in 1854 on the composition of *Hard Times*, Dickens declared "I am three parts mad, and the fourth, delirious, with perpetual rushing at Hard Times" (qtd. In Johnson 799).

Works Cited

Brooks, Peter. *Reading for the Piot*, New York: Knopf, 1984.

Bucknill, John Charles and Daniel H. Tuke. *A Manual of Psychological Medicine*. Philadelphia: 1958.

Castle, Robert. *The Regulation of Madness*. Trans. W.D. Halls. Berkeley: U of California Press, 1988.

Dickens, Charles. *A Tale of Two Cities*. New York: Penguin, 1991.

Foucault, Michel. *Discipline and Punish*. Trans. Alan Sheridan. New York: Vintage, 1977.

Hughes, Linda K. and Michael Lund. *The Victorian Serial*. Charlottesville: UP of Virginia, 1991.

CAROL HANBERY MACKAY
ON DICKENS, CARLYLE, AND RHETORIC

We know that Carlyle and Dickens are acutely, sometimes even painfully, aware of the separation of human minds not just because they expound upon this theme but because they demonstrate it in their portrayal of historical personages and fictional characters. Robespierre can serve to epitomize his unknowable separation for Carlyle. Calling upon him as a "hapless Chimera" and assigning him to the epithet of "seagreen ghost," Carlyle emphasizes the difficulty of knowing his thoughts, much less recreating him (FR, 3.6.6.274-275), but it is Robespierre's role as victim in fulfilling the prophecy of "the Revolution, like Saturn,...devouring its own children" (FR, 3.4.8.201) that ultimately confirms such separation and tragic misunderstanding. And Sydney Carton is, of course, Dickens' prime example of the isolated mind. Alone, unloved, castigated and self-castigating, Carton too is misunderstood. Yet it is precisely because Carton is so eloquent and expressive in soliloquy that we come to see the power of language to transcend the boundaries of human consciousness—even though those boundaries form barriers in the world that he physically inhabits.

Despite the fact that Carlyle declares that "no man can get himself explained" and that men are but "distorted phantasms" to one another, he tries to contact these ghosts of the past by evoking their physicality through violent rhetoric. Let us examine a typical evocation:

> On, then, all Frenchmen, that have hearts in your bodies! Roar with all your throats, of cartilage and metal, ye Sons of Liberty; stir spasmodically, whatsoever of utmost faculty is in you, soul, body, or spirit, for it is the hour! Smile, thou Louis Tournay, Cartwright of the Marais, old-soldier of the Regiment Dauphine; smile at that Outer Drawbridge chain, though the fiery hail whistles round thee! Never, over nave or felloe, did thy axe strike such a stoke. Down with it, man; down with it to Orcus: let the whole accursed Edifice sink thither, and Tyranny be swallowed up forever! Mounted, some say, on the roof of the guard-room, some "on bayonets stuck into joints of the wall," Louis Tournay smiles, brave Aubin Bonnemère (also an old solider) seconding him: the chain yields, breaks; the huge Drawbridge slam down, thundering (*avec fracas*). Glorious: and yet, alas, it is still but the outworks. The Eight grim Towers, with their Invalide musketry, their paving-stones and cannon-mouths, still soar aloft intact; Ditch yawning impassable, stone-faced; the inner Drawbridge with its back towards us: the Bastille is still to take! (FR, 1.5.6.190-191)

This passage initiates the typical Carlylean rhetorical pattern: it begins with an apostrophe, a direct address, as if to suggest that Carlyle is trying to break down ego and time boundaries. Then he invests his subject with physical detail, using violent imagery and his own disjointed Germanic rhetoric, as if to goad himself and us as much as the Frenchmen he seems to be inciting.[4] What follows is the kind of rhetoric that extends and magnifies—in his case, it pulls back to widen the scope and draw spatial parallels by multiplying the tower that remain to be taken.

Here we witness Carlyle employing incidents and characters as symbols: the people storming the prison represent his very effort to establish connections, to transcend barriers, (Interestingly enough, he underscores his skill by appearing to deny it: "To describe this Siege of the Bastille [thought to be one of the most important in History] perhaps transcends the talent of mortals"—FR, 1.56.191) Like Carlyle, Dickens too employs symbolism to describe the taking of the Bastille: heads, facades, mazes, the prison itself all point to isolation, while the surrounding ocean of the people of St. Antoine becomes an image of violent transcendence:[5]

> The sea of black and threatening waters, and of destructive upheaving of wave against wave, whose depths were yet unfathomed and whose forces were yet unknown. The remorseless ea of turbulently swaying shapes, voices of vengeance, and faces hardened in the furnaces of suffering until the touch of pity could make no mark on them. (TTC, 2.21.249)

By surrounding a symbol of isolation-the governor of the prison-the crowd highlights him as a representative of boundaries and separation. But it is Madame Defarge, "immovable" next to him and seeming to parallel him, who is the linking, transitional figure. It is her act of violence—the decapitation of the governor—that paradoxically unifies him with the group, now an "ocean of faces" in Dickens' rhetoric of transcendence.

From these two examples, we can begin to characterize the contrasting modes of rhetoric employed by both Carlyle and Dickens. The rhetoric of isolation usually involves a lone central figure, facades, solid boundaries, stillness, an absence of emotion, a sense of ineluctability that could only be disrupted by violence. In contrast, the rhetoric of transcendence employs multiple figures, parallels, reification, movement, emotion, foreshadowing that crosses boundaries of time and consciousness. This latter category encompasses the imagery of the abyss in man as well as his organic vision, which Albert J. LaValley traces back to Carlyle's "Characteristics" (1831) and *Sartor Resartus* (1833–1834)[6]. As for the transitional rhetoric— the rhetoric violence—it seems to gain momentum for Carlyle as The French Revolution proceeds; by the third volume, the historical violence that he repots is paralleled by his rhetoric until, in LaValley's terms, his response to the violence cases the work to become "riddled with ambivalent feelings, ambiguities, and contradictions."[7] Dickens on the other hand, succeeds in uniting the two opposing forms of rhetoric in Carton's last soliloquy: Carton is at once the lone emotionless figure and the prophet who sees beyond time and space.

Notes

4. In *Carlyle and His Era* (Santa Cruz, Calif. Dean E. McHenry Library, 1975), pp. 18, 19, Murray Baumgarten argues the interrelation between Carlyle's violent language and his method of perception. Technique and perception thus reflect each other as well as Carlyle's subject the modern world in the process of self merging.

5. For an accounting of the ocean as metaphor for the mob in both works, see Michael Goldberg, *Carlyle and Dickens* (Athens: University of Georgia Press, 1972) pp. 120-121.

6. See *Carlyle and the Idea of the Modern: Studies in Carlyle's Prophetic Literature and its Relation to Blake, Nietzsche, Marx, and Others* (New Haven: Yale University Press, 1968), pp. 127-129.

7. *Ibid.*, p. 159.

LEONARD MANHEIM
ON THE CHARACTER OF DR. MANETTE

The one remaining father-figure is the most interesting, complex, and well-developed character in the whole novel, Dr. Manette. Since he could not have been much more than twenty-five years old when hew as torn from his newly-wedded

English wife to be imprisoned in the Bastille for nearly eighteen years, he must have been less than forty-five when we first met him in Defarge's garret. And Dickens, let it be remembered, was forty-five when he wrote of him. Here is his portrait:

> A broad ray of light fell into the garret, and showed the workman with an unfinished shoe upon his lap, pausing in his labour. His few common tools and various scraps of leather were at his feet and on his bench. He had a white beard, raggedly cut, but not very long, a hollow face, and exceedingly bright eyes. The hollowness and thinness of his face would have caused them to look large, under his yet dark eyebrows and his confused white hair, though they had been really otherwise; but, they were naturally large, and looked unnaturally so. His yellow rags of shirt lay open at the throat, and showed his body to be withered and worn. (I, vi)

Of course the appearance of great age in a middle-age man is rationally explained by the suffering entailed by his long, unjust imprisonment. Yet, nearly eighteen years later (the repetition of the number is meaningful) when he has become the unwitting agent of his son-in-law's destruction and has been unable to use his special influences to procure Charles' release, he is pictured as a decayed mass of senility.

> "Who goes here? Whom have we within? Papers!"
> The papers are handed out and read.
> "Alexandre Manette. Physician. French. Which is he?"
> This is he; this helpless, inarticulately murmuring, wandering old man pointed out.
> "Apparently the Citizen-Doctor is not in his right mind? The Revolution fever will have been too much for him?"
> Greatly too much for him. (III, xiii)

Carton envisions his complete recovery, but we have some difficulty in believing it.

In the interim, however, he is pictured as a stalwart, middle-aged medical practitioner. His sufferings have caused a period of amnesia, with occasional flashes of painful recollection, as in the scene in which he hears of the discovery of a stone marked DIG in a cell in the Tower of London. We never know, by the way, whether his recollection at this moment is complete and whether he had, even furtively, any recall of the existence of the document of denunciation found by Mr. Defarge. The aspects of conscious and repressed memory are here handled with great skill by Dickens. Generally, his amnesia is reciprocal; he cannot recall his normal life during the period of relapse, or vice versa, especially when his relapses are triggered by events and disclosures which bring up memories of his old wrongs. His reversion to shoemaking for a short time after Charles proposes marriage to Lucie and again for a longer time following Lucie's marriage and Charles's final revelation of his long-suspected identity foreshadow the great disclosure which is to make him the unwitting aggressor against the happiness of his loving and beloved daughter.

When we consider Dr. Manette's conduct, however, we find that, whether Dickens consciously intended it to be or not, the doctor of Beauvais is a good psychiatrist, at least in the handling of his own illness. His shoemaking is superficially pictured as a symptom of mental regression and decay, but in its inception it must have been a sign of rebellion against madness rather than a symptom thereof. He relates that he begged for permission to make shoes as a means of diverting his mind from its unendurable suffering. Shoemaking, truly an example of vocational therapy, was the only contact with reality that his distracted mind, other wise cut from reality, possessed. It was, therefore, a means of bringing about his recovery. Lucie fears the shoemaking, but she realizes that her loving presence, coupled with the availability, if needed, of the vocational contact with reality, will serve to draw him back to normal adjustment. It would seem, then, that the act of Mr. Lorry and

Miss Pross, carried on furtively and guiltily, of destroying his shoemaker's bench and tools after his spontaneous recovery from the attack following Lucie's wedding, was a great error, an error against which the doctor, giving an opinion in the anonymous presentation of his own case by Mr. Lorry, strongly advises. For when he once again falls into a state of amnesia and confusion, after the realization of the change he has done to Charles and his impotence to remedy that damage, he calls for his bench and tools, but they are no longer to be had, and he huddles in a corner of the coach leaving Paris, a pitiful picture of mental decay from which we can see no hope of recovery despite the optimistic vision of Carton's last moments.

DAVID ROSEN ON THE ROOTS OF REVOLUTION

In *The Golden Bough*, first published some thirty years after *A Tale of Two Cities*, Sir James Frazer traces the genesis and morphology of ancient Mediterranean vegetation rites. As Frazer explains, Adonis, Attis, and Osiris were divine or semi-divine figures, whose violent deaths and miraculous rebirths insured the harvest's seasonal decay and growth. Since the fertility of the land was contingent on the well-being of these gods, a complex system of rituals was introduced to insure their strength:

> Men now attributed the annual cycle of change primarily to corresponding changes in their deities,...and thought that by performing certain magical rites they could aid the god who was the principle of life, in his struggle with the opposing principle of death. They imagined that they could recruit his failing energies and even raise him from the dead. (324)

Not surprisingly, these rituals typically involved the shedding of human blood, as persons were sacrificed in stead of the god. The Greek cult of Dionysus (the Roman Bacchus) was particularly colorful: like the Egyptian Osiris, Dionysus was cut to pieces by his enemies, only to rise reborn from the earth.

His worshipers, often in a state of wild intoxication, would devour their victim (in later years, a bull), after treating him to a similar demise. Frazer discusses the myth of Pentheus, familiar from Euripides' Bacchae:

> The [legend of Pentheus' death] may be...[a distorted reminiscence] of a custom of sacrificing divine kinds in the character of Dionysus and of dispersing the fragments of their broken bodies over the fields for the purpose of fertilizing them. It is probably no mere coincidence that Dionysus himself is said to have been torn to pieces at Thebes, the very place where according to the legend the same fate befell king Pentheus at the hands of the frenzied votaries of the vinegod.   (392)

Dickens, writing long before Frazer, seems to understand both the significance and the enduring power of such rituals; in his hands, the French revolution follows the pattern of pagan fertility rites.

The centuries of aristocratic rule have left France a wasteland. In the most palpable, physical sense, the rapacity of the nobility has emptied the national coffers, and left the countryside barren. The Parisian elite has the "truly noble idea, that the world was made for them. The text of [Monseigneur's order runs] "The earth and the fullness thereof are mine, saith Monseigneur" (135). As a result the provinces—and the Evremonde estate in particular—are desolate:

> Patches of poor rye where corn should have been, patches of poor peas and beans, patches of most coarse vegetable substitutes for wheat. On inanimate nature, as on the men and women who cultivated it, a prevalent tendency towards and appearance of vegetating unwillingly—a dejected disposition to give up, and wither away.   (143-44)

The blight is also spiritual and psychological. By attempting a sort of timeless permanence, and thus denying biology, the aristocratic ethos runs counter to normal, fertile human instinct. Monseigneur's drawing room is a menagerie wherein "charming grandmammas of sixty [dress and sup] as at twenty," and "it [is] hard to find...one solitary wife, who, in her manners and appearance, [would own] to being a mother" (137). The life of peasants is also unfruitful. In perhaps the novel's cruelest scene, soldiers play upon a common taboo and allow an executed man's blood to run into a village well, knowing that the community will be obliterated: "He is hanged there forty feet high—and is left hanging, poisoning the water....It is frightful, messieurs. How can the women and children draw water!" (201)[1] Within a few years, the Evremonde estate, formerly in decline, is empty:

> Far and wide lay a ruined country, yielding nothing but desolation. Every green leaf, every blade of grass and blade of grain, was as shriveled and poor as the miserable people. Everything was bowed down, dejected, oppressed and broken. Habitations, fences, domesticated animals, men, women, children and the soil that bore them—all worn out....Monseigneur had squeezed and wrung it,...had made edifying a paces of barbarous and barren wilderness. (256-57)

Dickens comments, in an ironic aside, that the aristocracy is "a great means of regeneration" (153); in the most ghoulish and literal sense possible, he is right. Even in their less bloodthirsty moments, the revolutionaries resemble Dionysian maenads.[2] The unearthly dance Darnay observes as he enters the country—

> After long and lonely spurring over dreary roads, they would come to a cluster of poor cottages, not steeped in darkness, but all glittering with lights, and would find the people, in a ghostly manner in the dead of night, circling hand in hand round a shrivelled tree of Liberty, or all drawn up together singing a Liberty song.

-expands later into the Carmagnole, a "dance of five thousand demons" (307). When the mob turns homicidal, its impulse is plainly cannibalistic, with it victims often torn limb from limb. Jacques Three, the most savage of Defarge's cohorts, is at Darnay's second trial a "life-thirsting, cannibal-looking, bloody-minded juror" (345). Later, he relishes the thought of Lucie's beheading: "Ogre that he was, he spoke like an epicure" (388).[3] After his first trial, Darnay is astonished by the affection of people who,

> carried by another current, would have rushed at him with the same intensity, to rend him to pieces and stew him over the streets. (314)

During the LaForce massacres, the murderers' "hideous countenances [are] all bloody and sweaty, awry with howling, and all staring with beastly excitement and want of sleep....Some women [hold] wine to their mouths that they might drink" (291). The "vortex" of the insurgence, naturally enough, is a wine-shop.

The long sequenced surrounding the death of Foulon brings the action closest to its primordial roots. As in Euripides' play, the most brutal Bacchantes are women. Dickens's paganism (starting with the Royal George pier-glass) is largely a matriarchal affair; here the reaction of the women to Foulon's discovery bears no trace of civilization (Gilbert 156):

> The drum was beating in the streets...and the Vengeance, uttering terrific shrieks, and flinging her arms about her head like all the forty Furies at once, was tearing from house to house, rousing the women. The men were terrible...but the women were a sight to chill the boldest...They ran out with streaming hair, urging one another, and themselves, to madness with the wildest cries and actions...With these cries, numbers of women, lashed into blind frenzy, whirled about, striking and tearing at

95

their own friends until they dropped into a passionate swoon, and were saved only by the men belonging to them from being trampled under foot. (252)

At the height of the delirium, the woman's deepest motive comes out:

> Give us the blood of Foulon, Give us the head of Foulon, Give us the heart of Foulon, Give us the body and soul of Foulon, *Rend Foulon to pieces, and dig him into the ground, that grass may grow from him.* (252, italics mine)

And so, he is dismembered, and his mouth stuffed with grass. As Dickens puts in, the Terror "has set a great mark of blood upon the blessed garnering time of harvest" (283).

Although pagan in origin, the revolutionaries' acts are disconcertingly close, formally, to Christian sacrament. As Frazer recognizes, both Christianity and vegetation cults commemorate, through the symbolic or literal consuming of flesh and drinking of blood, the sacrifice of a man-god whose death and resurrection have delivered the community (360, 481). Indeed, as the revolution progresses, it practices seem both to parallel and reverse those of Christianity. The first Parisian scene hints already that the confusion to come; the breaking of a wine-cask, at first a cause for celebration, gradually develops ominous, eucharistic overtones:

> Those who had been greedy with the staves of the cask, had acquired a tigerish smear about the mouth; and one tall joker so besmirched...scrawled upon a wall with his finger dipped in muddy wine-lees—BLOOD.
>
> The time was to come, when that wine too would be spilled on the street-stones, and when the stain of it would be red upon many there.

The insurrection takes hold, and the two fluids become almost interchangeable. At the grindstone, "what with dropping blood, and what with dropping wine...[all the murders'] wicked atmosphere seemed gore and fire" (291; Glancy 108-10). By the culmination of the novel, during the error, the sacrament has been perversely realized. At the scaffold, human "wine" is miraculously transformed into blood; tumbrils "carry the day's wine to La Guillotine" (399). In a brilliant extended metaphor, Dickens compares the Conciergerie's basement to a wine cellar:

> The Condemned...gentle born and peasant born; all red wine for La Guillotine, all daily brought into the light from the dark cellars of the loathsome prisons, and carried to her through the street to slake her devouring thirst.   (304)

The guillotine, as the official center of revolutionary ritual, is itself of course sanctified. First a "sharp female, newly born" (383), then "canonized" as the "Little Sainte Guillotine" (307), and finally a goddess, the "retributive instrument" (404) replaces the Cross as the symbol of, and means towards, national fruition.

> It was the sign of the regeneration of the human race. It superseded the Cross. Models of it were worn on breasts from which the Cross was discarded, and it was bowed down to and believed in where the Cross was denied.

Vegetation myths reach from the rebellion's faith, to annex the forms of Catholic worship (Glancy 117).

Notes

1. All page references to Charles Dickens, *A Tale of Two Cities*, ed. George Woodcock, London: Penguin, 1970.

2. Ewald Mengel discusses the blood Taboo in "The Poisoned Fountain: Dickens's Use of a Traditional Symbol in *A Tale of Two Cities*," *The Dickensian* 80, part 1 (Spring, 1984); 29. See also Frazer 227-30.

3. John Gross, "A Tale of Two Cities," *Dickens and the Twentieth Century*, ed. John Gross and Gabriel Pearson (Toronto: U of Toronto P, 1962) 193.

G.K. Chesterton
on Dickens's European Experience

For all practical purposes he had never been outside such places as Chatham and London. He did indeed travel on the Continent; but surely no man's travel was ever so superficial as his. He was more superficial than the smallest and commonest tourist. He went about Europe on stilts; he never touched the ground. There is one good test and one only of whether a man has traveled to any profit in Europe. An Englishman is, as such, a European, and as he approaches the central splendours of Europe he ought to feel that he is coming home. If he does not feel at home he had much better have stopped at home. England is a real home; London is a real home; and all the essential feelings of adventure of the picturesque can easily be gained by going out at night upon the flats of Essex or the cloven hills of Surrey. Your visit to Europe is useless unless it gives you the sense of an exile returning. Your first sight of Rome is futile unless you feel that you have seen it before. Thus useless and thus futile were foreign experiments and the continental raids of Dickens. He enjoyed them as he would have enjoyed, as a boy, a scamper out of Chatham into some strange meadows, as he would have enjoyed, when a grown man, a steam in a police boat out into the fens to the far east of London. But he was the Cockney venturing for; he was not the European coming home.

(...)

Dickens could not really conceive that there was any other city but his own.

It is necessary thus to insist that Dickens never understood the Continent, because only thus can we appreciate the really remarkable thing he did in *A Tale of Two Cities*. It is necessary to feel, first of all, the fact that to him London was the centre of the universe. He did not understand at all the real sense in which Paris is the capital of Europe. He had never realised that all roads lead to Rome. He had never felt (as an Englishman can feel) that he was an Athenian before he was a Londoner. Yet with everything against him he did this astonishing thing. He wrote a book about two cities, one of which he understood; the other he did not understand. And his description of the city he did not know is almost better than his description of the city he did know.

SYLVÈRE MONOD ON TYPES OF NARRATORS

In the case of A Tale of Two Cities it is obvious that there was an exceptionally close link between the book and the author, between the narrative and the man Charles Dickens, who asserted in his belief but striking preface that "throughout its execution, it has had complete possession of me" and significantly added: "I have so far verified what is one and suffered in these pages, as that I have certainly done and suffered it all myself." Even while making allowance for the writer's habitual overemphasis of his own emotional attitudes, his statements must be borne in mind; they imply that the usual distance or detachment from characters and tale could not be preserved entirely and even that the normal delegation from author to narrator could hardly be maintained throughout.

The bulk of the narrative, with the exceptions that must be called "intrusive," is delegated not to one but to several narrators, that is, to the teller of the tale or narrator proper, to a historian, and to a polemicist. The narrator occupies the position and exerts the privileges of omniscience, with some minor reservations as we shall see, but on the whole comfortably and unashamedly; he knows all that there is to be known about the characters and their thoughts and the course of events. The historian takes over whenever the knowledge required is not of private circumstances and fictional persons but of the real fate of two countries through a quarter of a century or more. A clear case of this substitution of the historian for the narrator occurs in book 1, chapter 5,[3] after the description of the wine-cask episode in the Paris suburb of Saint-Antoine. The street lamps in that area are said-presumably by such a contemporary observer as the narrator-to be swinging "in a sickly manner overhead, as if they were at sea." The very next sentence states, "Indeed they were at sea, and the ship and crew were in peril of tempest," a broader view of things and one that implies knowledge of the future as well as the present.

As for our third man, the polemicist, he is not so easily to be distinguished from the historian, for there is a satirical way of giving historical information that serves the purposes of both. The "Monseigneur" chapter (2.7) is neither straightforward narrative nor straightforward history: it is a kind of personalized satire that seems to rest on fragmentary or warped historical documentation. The aside about the Old Bailey and Bedlam (2.2) is satire in the guise of information; the allusion to "the last Louis but one, of the line that was never to break—the fourteenth Louis" (2.9) is again polemical history. What the three narrators have in common is their undisguised omniscience, even though it varies in degree, as does the distance between them and the tale or the characters.

Note

3. The numbers given after each quotation hereafter in my text likewise refer to book and chapter numbers of the *Tale*.

JOHN KUCICH ON FORMS OF VIOLENCE IN THE NOVEL

The psychological dynamic here is specified by Hegel's Master—Slave dialectic: the Master is he who is most willing to give up his life for a greater, intangible good—a transcendent good not restricted by the economic taint of mere worldly survival. The Slave, then, is he who opts for survival rather than risking his life in a fight with the Master. In Hegel's dialectic, however, if the Master proves his greater willingness to face violent death and then survives because of the Salve's capitulation, this proved capacity for totalizing violence becomes the emblem and the instrument of his successful domination. The Master thus becomes trapped in petty factualism when he seeks to make his transcendent liberation—proved through his willingness to die violently—endure in the form of the Slave's recognition of that transcendent violence. Consequently, there are two possible ways in which violence may be exorcised: first, as a spontaneous release from slavishness through self-regardless violence—which, in temporal terms, is "pure" but also "meaningless" because it is not designated to be profitable—second, as a calculated retreat from self-abandonment toward the use of violence against others in an attempt to make one's transcendent liberation endure in the world. In terms of Dickens's novel, any desire for extremity that stops short of self-annihilation becomes impure by being implicated in the temporal arena of rivalry: most obviously, the mob projects violence outwards to preserve itself while affirming its claim to the righteousness and the transcendence implied by its willingness to confront death.

In *A Tale of Two Cities*, Hegel's two dialectical forms of violence are personified and set at war with each other. The purity of self-violence clearly belongs at first to the lower classes, who "held life as of no account, and were demented with a passionate readiness to sacrifice it" (bk. 2, chap. 21). Thus, the concrete effects of the revolutionaries' violence as an annihilation of their humanity—and, therefore, a violation of their human limitations—are actualized before us: we witness the transformation of rational figures like the Defarge couple into maddened beasts during the storming of the Bastille. Furthermore, to emphasize the "unnatural" and "non-human" element in the revolutionaries' passion, Dickens made their spokesperson a woman, since, in Dickens's world, the supreme disruption of normal expectations about human nature is an absence of tenderness in women. In the Parisian violence, even la Guillotine is female. And to heighten his effect, Madame Defarge's knitting in service of violence is set in sharp contrast to Lucie Manette's "golden thread" of pacification and harmony, as well as to the "domestic arts" that Lucie had learned in Madame Defarge's France. Most importantly, this yearning for the pure release of self-violence is identified as the ultimate form of desire for freedom through the good characters: Darnay, on his last night in prison, becomes fascinated with the guillotine—he has "a strong besetting desire to know what to do when the time came; a desire gigantically disproportionate to the few swift moments to which it referred; a wondering that was more like the wondering of some other spirit within his, than his own" (bk. 3, chap. 3). At one point, too, the narrator isolates the mob's fascination with the pure release of violent death, and makes of it a common human desire: "a species of fervor or intoxication, known, without doubt, to have led some persons to brace the guillotine unnecessarily, and to die by it, was not mere boastfulness, but a wild infection of the wildly shaken public mind. In seasons of pestilence, some of us will have a secret attraction to the disease-a terrible passing inclination to die of it. And all of us have like wonders hidden in our breasts, only needing circumstances to evoke them" (bk. 3, chap. 6). Thoughts like this lend a new resonance to the chapter title "Drawn to the Loadstone Rock," a chapter in which Darnay decides—for seemingly rational reasons, though he does refuse to discuss them with anyone who might restrain him—to go back to France, and help stress the novel's movement toward some kind of willed self-destruction.

The liberating intentions behind the lower classes' violence, however, are only a response to the repressive image of non-human freedom and "represented" violence that define the power of the class of Monseigneur. Instead of being defined through overt acts of violence, life among the upper classes revolves around static representations of their non-humanity—emblems of their willingness to violate human limits. The Marquis's own non-humanity marks itself in his freedom from emotion—the narrator at one point describes his appearance as being "a fine mask" (bk. 2, chap. 9), and his face is compared to the stone faces of his gargoyles. In his conversation with Charles, he annihilates feeling through the codified formality of manners: "the uncle made a graceful gesture of protest, which was so clearly a slight form of good breeding that it was not reassuring" (bk. 2, chap. 9). Generally, the hallmark of status among the Marquis's class is this "leprosy of unreality" (bk. 2, chap. 7). The Fancy Ball, for example, is full of "Unbelieving Philosophers," who construct elaborately meaningless verbal structures, and "Unbelieving Chemists," who have their eyes on alchemy—both are in pursuit of the unnatural, through words or through metals. Good breeding itself "was at that remarkable time—and has been since—to be known by its fruits of indifference to every natural subject of human interest." Once again, too, the contrast is clearest in the image of the female; among the women of the Marquis's society, their chief distinction is their escape from maternity: it was "hard to discover among the angels of that sphere one solitary wife, who, in her manners and appearance, owned to being a Mother....Peasant women kept the unfashionable babies close, and brought them up, and charming grandmammas of sixty dressed up and supped as at twenty."

There is a violence among the Marquis's class, of course, but it is colder, and has a clear function as a representation: that is, their violence is merely an occasional symbol of the mastery of the rich, since it proves their right to waste lives if they choose to-the lives of the lower orders. When the Marquis asserts that running down children with his carriage is a right of his station, he takes no passionate satisfaction from the killing; he takes only a numbed confirmation of his status. Initially, when the rebels in *A Tale of Two Cities* kill, they kill in passion, while the rich kill as spectacle—as, for example, when the royal government executes the murderer of the Marquis and leaves him hanging forty feet in the air. The Marquis expresses this functionality of violence explicitly; when Charles complains that his family is hated in France for their cruelty, the Marquis answers: "Let us hope so....Detestation of the high is the involuntary homage of the low" (bk. 2, chap. 9).

The Hegelian horror of *A Tale of Two Cities* is this: at the point when the revolutionaries stop short of their own willingness to brave death and attempt to make their release permanent and meaningful in the form of a Republic, they trap themselves in the reified form of diverted violence—the petty, mechanical, and cruel contortions of human rivalry. We lost sympathy for the rebels when they lose sight of their limitless freedom—their "pure" release—and become trapped in their own revenge, thus imitating their oppressors. The very name of Madame Defarge's companion is "The Vengeance," and Madame Defarge undercuts herself through an ironic imitation: she dedicates herself to destroying the innocent Darnay family just as her own innocent family was destroyed. More disturbingly, for Madame Defarge, as for the rest of the revolutionaries, passionate revenge gives way to the invention of spurious rivalry, the murder of innocent victims. The purely mechanical quality of his imitative violence is underscored by the ominous note of historical destiny in this novel: the continuous references to things "running, their courses" and the metaphors of echoing footsteps and approaching thunderstorms. In Dickens's novel, the "pure" wish for release always becomes tainted when it is diverted away from the self, and when the limits that are violated become the limits of others.

JOHN FORSTER ON DICKENS AND STORYTELLING

A letter of the following month expresses the intention he had when he began the story, and in what respect it differs as to method from all his other books. Sending in proof four numbers ahead of the current publication, he adds: "I hope you will like them. Nothing but the interest of the subject, and the pleasure of striving with the difficulty of the form of treatment, —nothing in the way of mere money, I mean,—could else repay the time and trouble of the incessant condensation. But I set myself the little task of making *a picturesque story*, rising in every chapter, with characters true to nature, but whom the story should express more than they should express themselves by dialogue. I mean in other words, that I fancied a story of incident might be written (in place of the odious stuff that is written under that pretence), pounding the characters in its own mortar, and beating their interest out of them. If you could have read the story all at once, I hope you wouldn't have stopped halfway."* Another of his letters supplies the last illustration I need to give of the design and meanings in regard to this tale expressed by himself. It was a reply to some objections of which the principal were, a doubt if the feudal cruelties came sufficiently within the date of the action to justify his use of them, and some question as to the manner of disposing of the chief revolutionary agent in the plot. "I had of course full knowledge of the formal surrender of the feudal privileges, but these had been bitterly felt quite as near to the time of the Revolution as the Doctor's narrative, which you will remember dates long before the Terror. With the slang of the new philosophy on the one side, it was surely not unreasonable or unallowable, on the other, to suppose a nobleman wedded to the old cruel ideas, and representing the time going out as his nephew represents the time coming in. If there be anything certain on earth, I take it that the condition of the French peasant generally at that day was intolerable. No later inquiries or provings by figures will hold water against the tremendous testimony of men living at the time. There is a curious book printed at Amsterdam, written to make out no case whatever, and tiresome enough in its literal dictionary-like minuteness; scattered up and down the pages of which is full authority for my marquis. This is Mercier's *Tableau de Paris*. Rousseau is the authority for the peasant's shutting up his house when he had a bit of meat. The tax-tables are the authority for the wretched creature's impoverishment....I am not clear, and I never have been clear, respecting the canon of fiction which forbids the interposition of accident in such a case as Madame Defarge's death. Where the accident is inseparable from the passion and action of the character; where it is strictly consistent with the entire design, and arises out of some culminating proceeding on the part of the individual which the whole story has led up to; it seems to me to become, as it were, an act of divine justice. And when I use Miss Pross (though this is quite another question) to bring about such a catastrophe, I have the positive intention of making that half-comic intervention a part of the desperate woman's failure; and of opposing that mean death, instead of a desperate one in the streets which she wouldn't have minded, to the dignity of Carton's. Wrong or right, this was all design, and seemed to me to be in the fitness of things."

These are interesting intimations of the care with which Dickens worked; and there is no instance in his novels, excepting this, of a deliberate and planned departure from the method of treatment which had been pre-eminently the source of his popularity as a novelist. To rely less upon character than upon incident, and to resolve that his actors should be expressed by the story more than they should express themselves by dialogue, was for him a hazardous, and can hardly be called an entirely successful, experiment. With singular dramatic vivacity, much constructive art, and with descriptive passages of a high order everywhere (the dawn of the terrible outbreak in the journey of the marquis from Paris to his country seat, and the London crowd at the funeral of the spy, may be instanced for their power), there was probably never a book by a great humourist, and an artist so prolific in the conception of character, with so little humour and so few rememberable figures. Its merits lie elsewhere. Though there are excellent traits and touches all through the revolutionary scenes, the only full-length that stands out prominently is the picture of the wasted life saved at last by heroic sacrifice. Dickens speaks of his design to make impressive the dignity of Carton's death, and in this he succeeded perhaps even beyond his expectation. Carton suffers himself to be mistaken for another, and gives his life that the girl he loves may be happy with that other; the secret being known only to a poor little girl in the tumbril that takes them to the scaffold, who at the moment has discovered it, and whom it strengthens also to die. The incident is beautifully told; and it is at least only fair to set against verdicts not very favourable as to this effort of his invention, what was said of the particular character and scene, and of the book generally, by an American critic whose literary studies had most familiarized him with the rarest forms of imaginative writing. "Its portrayal of the noble-natured castaway makes it almost a peerless book in modern literature, and gives it a place among the highest examples of literary art....The conception of this character shows in its author an ideal of magnanimity and of charity unsurpassed. There is not a grander, lovelier figure than the self-wrecked, self-devoted Sydney Carton, in literature or history; and the story itself is so noble in its spirit, so grand and graphic in its style, and filled with a pathos so profound and simple, that it deserves and will surely take a place among the great serious works of imagination." I should myself prefer to say that its distinctive merit is less in any of its conceptions of character, even Carton's, than as a specimen of Dickens's power in imaginative story-telling. There is no piece of fiction known to me, in which the domestic life of a few simple private people is in such a manner knitted and interwoven with the outbreak of a terrible public event, that the one seems but part of the other. When made conscious of the first sultry drops of a thunderstorm that fall upon a little group sitting in an obscure English lodging, we are witness to the actual beginning of a tempest which is preparing to sweep away everything in France. And, to the end, the book in this respect is really remarkable.

Notes

* The opening of this letter (August 25th, 1859), referring to a conviction for murder, afterwards reversed by a Home Office pardon against the continued and steadily expressed opinion of the judge who tried the case, is too characteristic of the writer to be lost. "I cannot easily tell you how much interested I am by what you tell me of our brave and excellent friend....I have often had more than half a mind to write and thank that upright judge. I declare to heaven that I believe such a service one of the greatest that a man of intellect and courage can render to society....Of course I have been driving the girls out of their wits here, incessantly proclaiming that there needed no medical evidence either way, and that the case was plain without it....Lastly, of course, though a merciful man (because a merciful man, I mean) I would hang any Home Secretary, Whig, Tory, Radical, or otherwise, who should step in between so black a scoundrel and the gallows....I am reminded of Tennyson that King Arthur would have made short work of the amiable man! How fine the *Idylls* are! Lord! What a blessed thing it is to read a man who really can write. I thought nothing could be finer than the first poem, till I came to the third; but when I had read the last, it seemed to me absolutely unapproachable." Other literary likings rose and fell with him, but he never faltered in his allegiance to Tennyson.

ANDREW SAUNDERS ON DICKENS AND PARIS

The excitingly untidy Paris he encountered at some length in the 1840s not only complemented his generally unflattering picture of London, it remained for him a city of enthralling contrasts. If, on one level, he could boldly proclaim in one of his Uncommercial essays that 'No Englishman knows what gaslight is, until he sees the Rue De Rivoli and the Palais Royal after dark he generally held a less dazzled opinion of Parisians.[55] The French, his often ambiguous letters home indicate, seemed 'frightfully civil, and grotesquely extortionate' and Paris itself both 'as bright, and as wicked, and as wanton, as ever' and 'a wicked and detestable place, though wonderfully attractive' which was the best summed up in Hogarth's 'unmentionable' phrase 'gilt and b—sh—t'.[56] In January 1847, however, he wrote to John Forster in a gushing schoolboy French describing the people amongst whom he was living as 'la nation la plus grande et la plus noble, et la plus merveilleuse, du monde' and signed himself with a flourish as "CHARLES DICKENS, Français naturalisé, et Citoyen de Paris".[57]

The sense of novelty informed by anomaly was to continue to mould both his feeling for Paris and his attempts to characterize the city. In two pieces written much later in his career, the essay 'A Flight' (*Household Words*, 1857, later included in *Reprinted Pieces* in 1858) and the Christmas Story, *Mrs. Lirriper's Legacy* (*All the Year Round*, 1864), Paris retains its atmosphere of excitement but it is now and excitement tinged with magic. Unlike the disillusioned visitors to the cramped heart of the city in the early part of the century, the London lodging-house keeper, Emma Lirriper, finds the Paris of the 1860s 'town and country both in one, and carved stone and long streets of high houses and gardens and fountains and statues and trees and gold...and clean table-cloths spread everywhere for dinner and people sitting out of doors smoking and sipping all day...and every shop a completed and elegant room, and everybody seeming to play at everything in this world. She is especially struck by 'the sparkling lights...after dark' and by 'the crowed of theatres and the crowd of people and the crowd of all sorts, it's pure enchantment'. The feeling of 'enchantment' is shared by Dickens's narrator in "A Flight', a gentleman visitor to Paris overwhelmed by the speed with which modern traveler can cross from run-of-the-mill England to exotic France. The South Eastern Railway Company has, he claims, realized the wild dreams of the Arabian Nights 'in these prose days', whisking travelers from one civilization to the next as if in a dream. Yet this dream of the Paris of the Second Empire, the 'ville lumière,' is a bewitching reality confirmed by a walking through the first *arrondissement*:

> The crowds in the streets, the lights in the shops and balconies, the elegance, variety and beauty of their decoration, the number of the theatres, the brilliant cafes with their windows thrown up high and their vivacious groups at little tables on the pavement, the light and glitter of the houses turned as it were inside out, soon convince me that it is no dream; that I am in Paris, howsoever I got here. I stroll down to the sparkling Palais Royal, up the Rue de Rivoli, to the Place Vendome....I walk up to the Barriere de l'Etoile, sufficiently dazed by my flight to have a pleasant doubt of the reality of everything about me; of the lively crowed, the overhanging trees, the performing dogs, the hobby-horses, the beautiful perspectives of shining lamps: the hundred and one enclosures where the singing is, in gleaming orchestras of azure and gold, and where star-eyed Houri comes round with a box for voluntary offerings.

Dickens's London is never like this. It is never so glittering, never so at ease with itself, never so essentially frivolous and fantastic.

Yet Paris retained its dark side in Dickens's imagination. Since John Carey drew particular attention to the essays in his *The Violent Effigy* (1973), The Uncommercial Traveller's visits to the Paris Morgue have been taken to justify the assertion that Dickens 'never missed a human carcass if he could help it'.[58] The two essays in question ('Travelling Abroad' and "Some Recollections of Morality', both 1863) certainly suggest that the Morgue held a compulsively gloomy fascination for Dickens, a nightmarish fascination which might be seen as running counter to the otherwise dream-like impression made by Paris. In the first essay, the Uncommercial, who is generally much preoccupied with death, confesses that whenever he is in Paris he is 'dragged by invisible force into the Morgue. He even admits to visiting it one Christmas Day. In the second, which opens with a brief account of Haussmann's radical clearances on the Île de la Cité (for some new wonder in the way of public Street, Place, Garden, Fountain, or all four'), the narrator turns from mutability to morality and broods on the adjacent Morgue, on its exposed cadavers, and on the indifferent Parisians who come to gawp at them. Although Dickens undoubtedly was, as Carey puts it, both 'intrigued by dead bodies' and imaginatively stimulated by them, it should be remembered that the Morgue was one of the customary sights of Paris, prominently and centrally situated, recommended by guide books, drawn by artists, and visited by curious foreign visitors and passing Parisians alike.[59] Dickens was not necessarily abnormal, at least by the standards of his own time, in sarily abnormal, at least by the standards of his own time, in feeling himself repeatedly compelled to view its macabre exhibits. What is of significance here is precisely why Dickens should be so prone to recollections of morality in 'glittering' 'enchanted' Paris. In some vital ways, I would suggest the greatest anomaly that Dickens felt to be present in modern Paris was that this same brightly lit, wondrously mutable, city of pleasure coexisted with vivid memories of its recent bloody history.

Notes:

55.'The Boiled Beef of New England.'

56. *Letters*, Pilgrim Edition, iv. 661; 665–6; 669.

57. Ibid. v. 5 (Jan. 1847).

58. John Carey, *The Violent Effigy: A Study of Dickens' Imagination* (1973; 2nd edn. 1991) 81.

59. The Morgue was, for example, visited by Thomas Hardy and his new bride on their honeymoon and is taken in as part of a Sunday afternoon stroll along the Seine by the young artists in du Maurier's *Trilby*. It also memorably appears as a sight of Paris in Zola's *Thérèse Raquin*. For Dickens and the Morgue see also Andrew Sanders, *Charles Dickens: Resurrectionist* (1982), 46–7. The Morgue was recommended to visitors by Galignani's *New Paris Guide* (1842), 58, though by 1890 Murray's *Hand-Book for Visitors to Paris* would remark with distaste the existence of 'a perpetual stream of men, women and children [who] pour in an out of this horrible exhibition, to gaze at the hideous objects before them, usually with great indifference' (249–50).

Works by Charles Dickens

"A Dinner at Poplar Walk," 1833.

Sketches by Boz, 1836.

Pickwick Papers, 1836–1837.

Oliver Twist, 1837–1839.

Nicholas Nickelby, 1838–1839.

The Old Curiosity Shop, 1840–1841.

Barnaby Rudge, 1841.

American Notes, 1842.

A Christmas Carol, 1843.

Martin Chuzzlewit, 1843–1844.

The Chimes, 1844.

The Cricket on the Hearth, 1845.

The Battle of Life, 1846.

Pictures from Italy, 1846.

Dombey and Son, 1846–1848.

The Haunted Man, 1848.

David Copperfield, 1849–1850.

A Child's History of England, 1851–1853.

Bleak House, 1852–1853.

Hard Times, 1854.

Little Dorrit, 1855–1857.

A Tale of Two Cities, 1859.

Great Expectations, 1861.

Our Mutual Friend, 1864–1865.

The Mystery of Edwin Drood, 1870.

Annotated Bibliography

Baldridge, Cates. "Alternatives to Bourgeois Individualism in *A Tale of Two Cities." Studies in English Literature* 30:4:633-655.

Baldridge proposes that while Dickens certainly experienced ambivalence towards the Revolution, which consolidated the power of the masses, he used *A Tale of Two Cities* to express his unease about his own individualistic, Industrial Revolution–era system.

Brannan, Robert Louis, ed. *Under the Management of Mr. Charles Dickens: His Production of "The Frozen Deep."* Ithaca, New York: Cornell University Press, 1966.

Includes the text of the Wilkie Collins play that inspired Dickens to write *A Tale of Two Cities.* Brannan's thorough introduction gives us a provocative picture of Dickens at the time of the play, which finished its run one year before the publication of *Two Cities*—as a man, an editor, an actor, and a businessman.

Carey, John. *The Violent Effigy: A Study of Dickens's Imagination* (2nd Edition). London: Faber and Faber, 1991.

A profoundly important book that examines Dickens's works through his use of the macabre and grotesque. Among other things, Carey covers corpses, coffins, and grave robberies. His work enables us to appreciate not only the horror of *A Tale of Two Cities*, but also its humor.

Carlyle, Thomas, *The French Revolution.* First published by J.M. Dent: London, 1837. Everyman's Library: New York, last reprint 1980.

The history of the French Revolution that influenced *A Tale of Two Cities.* Carlyle envisioned the Revolution as a natural disaster, and the language he employs to describe it, "sea," "earthquake," and "storm," are the words that Dickens borrows for his novel. Dickens also paraphrases entire

Carlyle paragraphs, most significantly in his descriptions of the storming of the Bastille.

Chesterton, G.K. "A Tale of Two Cities." *Appreciations and Criticisms of the Works of Charles Dickens.* New York: Haskell House Publications, 1970: 188-196.

Chesterton's discussion of *A Tale of Two Cities* is primarily geographical. Dickens was a quintessentially British writer; although he had traveled to France, his understanding of that country, and others, was limited to that of a superficial tourist. Chesterton argues that just as Dickens felt trapped in his life, so he felt trapped in England. By taking his narrative to France, he hoped to be able to conquer his personal inertia.

Chisick, Harvey. "Dickens's Portrayal of the People in *A Tale of Two Cities*." *The European Legacy*, no. 5, 2000: 645–661.

A discussion of Dickens's attitude towards the lower classes in the novel.

Collins, Philip. "A Tale of Two Novels: *A Tale of Two Cities* and *Great Expectations* in Dickens' Career." *Dickens Studies Annual 2.* Carbondale: Southern Illinois University Press, 1972: 336–351.

Collins compares the critical receptions of *A Tale of Two Cities* and the book that immediately followed, *Great Expectations*, and comments on the irony. For while Dickens called *A Tale of Two Cities* "his best story," it was universally panned. *Great Expectations*, on the other hand, which Dickens approached with reticence, was considered one of his best works.

———. *Dickens and Crime* (3rd edition). London: Macmillan and St. Martin's Press, 1994.

A seminal work in which Collins investigates Dickens's obsession with justice system, enhancing his arguments with historical facts. Considering the key role that the courts play in *A Tale of Two Cities*, the book provides interesting insights.

The first chapter, "Dickens and His Age," gives perspective into how Dickens may have exaggerated the courtroom atrocities he so frequently portrayed. "The Punishment of Death" is relevant when one considers the gory capital punishments doled out during the course of the novel, and the chapter "The Separate System—Philadelphia and the Bastille" analyzes Dickens's vision of the French courts.

Dickens Studies Annual: Essays on Victorian Fiction, 12. New York: AMS Press, 1983.

Volume 12 of the *Dickens Studies Annual* has a number of essays dedicated to *A Tale of Two Cities.* Among the essays of note: Alfred D. Hutter's essay on Dickens's morbid obsessions; Carol Hanbery MacKay's discussion of Dickens and Carlyle and their use of the omniscient, prophetic voice; Eigner's analysis of the oft-overlooked character of Charles Darnay as rebel, everyman, problematic romantic hero; and Catherine Gallagher's discussion on how resurrection functions as a narrative double to execution and revolution, and as a double to itself—good resurrection versus bad.

Engel, Monroe. "Addenda: The Sports of Plenty." *The Maturity of Dickens.* Cambridge: Harvard University Press. 1959: 169–189.

A discussion of *Hard Times, A Tale of Two Cities,* and *The Mystery of Edwin Drood,* which stand out from the rest of Dickens's later works not only for their length, but for their dogmatism. Engel dismisses much of *A Tale of Two Cities,* but he does offer a few points of interest. He criticizes the novel's lack of dramatic punch by comparing its critical scenes to similar ones in *Bleak House* and *Great Expectations,* notably those that take place in the courtroom. Like many critics, Engel believes that the novel's strength lies in its theme of death and resurrection.

Stephen, Sir James Fitzjames. "A Tale of Two Cities." First published in *Saturday Review,* 17 December 1859, pp.

741–43. Reprinted in George H. Ford and Lauriat Lane, Jr., (ed.) *The Dickens Critics*. Ithaca, New York: Cornell University Press, 1961.

A damning and rather witty review of the novel by one of Dickens's contemporaries, who criticizes it as "grotesque and pathetic," citing its melodramatic characters and dialogue, and in particular, Dickens's clumsy attempt to capture the French speech in English.

Forster, John. *The Life of Charles Dickens*. London: Cecil Palmer, 1928. Edited and annotated with an introduction by J.W.T. Ley.

This is the first major biography of Dickens, written by his friend John Forster, who had access to Dickens's friends and family, and also his correspondence. His chapter on *A Tale of Two Cities* (pp. 729–732) draws heavily on Dickens's journals and letters while he was writing the novel and provides a glimpse of the author's perspective.

Glancy, Ruth. *A Tale of Two Cities: Dickens's Revolutionary Novel*. Boston: Twayne's Masterwork Series, 1991.

A thorough introduction to *A Tale of Two Cities*, which examines its historical context, as well as character development, symbolism, the backdrops of France and England, and recurring patterns of imagery. Of particular interest are Glancy's chapter, "The Setting: England," where she compares Miss Pross and Madame Defarge, and "The Doctor of Beauvais," which is devoted to a portrait of Doctor Manette.

Gold, Joseph. *Charles Dickens: Radical Moralist*. Minnesota: University of Minneapolis Press, 1972.

A social and political analysis of the works of Charles Dickens. The chapter on *A Tale of Two Cities*, entitled "The Resurrection and the Life," discusses the novel as at once one of Dickens's most radical works, and at the same time one of his most optimistic. By blurring the lines between history and mythology, Gold argues, Dickens takes a severe stance on political corruption while still offering up the possibility of redemption at the end.

Goldberg, Michael. *Carlyle and Dickens.* Athens: University of Georgia Press, 1972.

An analysis of the influence of historian Thomas Carlyle upon his contemporary and friend Charles Dickens. Goldberg's argument is compromised mainly of quotes from both authors which illustrate where Dickens borrowed from Carlyle.

Gross, John. "*A Tale of Two Cities.*" John Gross and Gabrielle Pearson, eds. *Dickens and the Twentieth Century.* Toronto: University of Toronto Press, 1962: 187–198.

It is interesting that Gross, the editor of this volume, which is composed of analyses of Dickens's individual novels arranged in chronological order, should select *A Tale of Two Cities* as his novel of choice. With an engaging style, Gross, a theatrical and literary critic, focuses on the recurring themes and life and death, resurrection and redemption, concluding with a debate about whether the novel's ending is indeed as happy as most critics claim.

Hollington, Michael. "The Grotesque in History: *Barnaby Rudge* and *A Tale of Two Cities.*" *Dickens and the Grotesque.* Beckenham, England: Croom Helm, 1984: 96–122.

Hollington's chapter is yet another discussion on Dickens's use of the grotesque—from coffins to corpses to coffin diggers, in which he argues that the historical setting of *A Tale of Two Cities* allows Dickens liberty to explore the macabre images that he so loved.

Johnson, Edgar. *Charles Dickens: His Tragedy and Triumph.* New York: Simon and Schuster, 1952.

Johnson's biography of Charles Dickens is generally acknowledged to be one of the best. His chapter "Track of a Storm," (vol. 2) relates the turbulent circumstances in Dickens's life that helped give rise to *A Tale of Two Cities.*

The chapter "The Tempest and the Ruined Garden" analyzes the novel in more depth, as well as discussing the particular aspects of the French Revolution that attracted the author.

Kucich, John. "The Purity of Violence: *A Tale of Two Cities.*" *Dickens Studies Annual* 8. New York: AMS Press, 1980.

Kucich argues that the strength of *A Tale of Two Cities* is in its uncompromising—and pure—vision of death and violence.

Lamb, John B. "Domesticating History: Revolution and Moral Management in *A Tale of Two Cities.*" *Dickens Studies Annual* 25. New York: AMS Press, 1996: 227–224.

An analysis that equates the sexuality of the novel with its portrayal of political unrest. The Revolution and Madame Defarge represent "deviant femininity," or feminine power that is out of control, which domestic femininity, as represented by Lucie, must overcome.

Manheim, Leonard. "A Tale of Two Characters: A Study in Multiple Projections." *Dickens Studies Annual* 1. Carbondale: Southern Illinois University Press, 1970: 225–237.

Manheim's excellent essay examines the idea of character doubling and multiplicity in *A Tale of Two Cities*. However, what makes the essay interesting is its compassionate discussion of Dr. Manette, whose personal strengths have so often been overlooked. In his alternating states of madness and sanity, Manette functions as his own double; he is both his savior and betrayer and is perhaps, as Manheim argues, the most heroic man in the book.

Marcus, David D. "The Carlylean Vision of *A Tale of Two Cities.*" *Studies in the Novel* 8, no. 1. Northern Texas State University, 1976: 56–69.

A discussion of Carlyle's influence on *A Tale of Two Cities* which focuses on what Carlyle called "natural superhumanism," or the Romantic desire to understand the divine in secular terms. Carlyle, by equating the Revolution to both a natural catastrophe and an act of God, has also been able to explain the religious experience in humane, factual, and hence graspable way.

Monod, Sylvère. "Dickens's Attitudes in *A Tale of Two Cities.*" In Ada Nisbet and Blake Nevius, eds. *Dickens Centennial Essays*, Berkeley: University of California Press, 1971: 166–183.

Monod offers a formalistic approach by discussing Dickens's relationship as narrator to the novel.

Morgentaler, Goldie. *Dickens and Heredity: When Like Begets Like.* London: Macmillan Press, 2000.

A discussion of Dickens's works premised on genetics, and on whether his characters actually inherit their moral traits. Morgentaler's discussion of *A Tale of Two Cities* is particularly relevant—Darnay is condemned for the crimes of his uncle and father—but the question remains whether he is an actual heir to their villainy. Dickens resolves this by making Darnay and Sidney Carton twins. If two men unrelated by blood can be so similar, Darnay may not have inherited the sins of his natural ancestors.

Oddie, William. *Dickens and Carlyle: The Question of Influence.* London: Centenary, 1972.

Oddie's book is more analytical than David D. Marcus's, and also more critical. He concludes that Dickens's use of Carlyle in the novel is superficial, and actually betrays a fundamental misunderstanding of the historian.

Petch, Simon. "The Business of Barrister in *A Tale of Two Cities.*" *Criticism* 44:1:27–42.

Petch begins by discussing Sidney Carton in terms of his role as a lawyer, but eventually extends his essay to include an analysis of the professional roles played by other major characters, such as Stryver and Doctor Manette.

Phillips, Watts. *The Dead Heart.* 1859; first performed at the New Adelphi Theatre on November 10, 1859.

According to the biographer Peter Ackroyd, the producer Benjamin Webster read a draft of Watts's play, which is set during the French Revolution, while Dickens was recovering from "The Frozen Deep." (Ackroyd, 777) Its ending, in which the hero goes to the guillotine in the place of the son of the woman he loves, is notably similar to that of *A Tale of Two Cities*.

Rosen, David. "*A Tale of Two Cities*: Theology of Revolution." *Dickens Studies Annual* 27. New York: AMS Press, 1997: 171–185.

Rosen's essay is a fascinating examination of the Christian and pagan echoes in the novel, which refers to such easily recognizable classics as the New Testament and *The Golden Bough*.

Sanders, Andrew. "Telling of Two Cities." *Dickens and the Spirit of the Age*. Oxford: Oxford University Press, 1999.

A socioeconomic analysis of *A Tale of Two Cities* that examines the novel through commentators like Frederick Engels and historical statistics that illustrate the urban conditions of nineteenth-century Paris and London. Saunders argues that the Paris that Dickens wrote was one he knew from books only, at odds with the actual city. Ironic, as Dickens thought himself a relentless reporter.

Schama, Simon. *Citizens*. New York: Alfred A. Knopf, 1989.

One of the most respected accounts of the French Revolution to come out in recent years. Engaging, anecdotal, and easy to read, it is nevertheless more tempered than Thomas Carlyle's account, and includes in its investigation the intellectual movements that were behind French Revolution, as well as the violence.

Schor, Hilary. "Novels of the 1850s: *Hard Times, Little Dorrit,* and *A Tale of Two Cities*." John O. Jordan, ed. *The Cambridge Companion to Charles Dickens*. Cambridge: Cambridge University Press, 2001: 64–77.

Schor approaches Dickens's 1850s works as social critiques. Among the three novels she discusses, she argues that *A Tale of Two Cities* is his most idealistic. It is his utopian novel, one that, although written in the spirit of social unease, offers the reader the promise of the redemptive powers of history.

Sroka, Kenneth M. "A Tale of Two Gospels: Dickens and John." *Dickens Studies Annual 27*, New York: AMS Press, 1997: 145–169.

Sroka discusses the influence of the Gospel of St. John, which is the text that Sidney Carton famously quotes at the end, "I am the Resurrection and the Life." Like St. John, Carton, he argues, by dying resurrects not only himself; he also resurrects history from the disaster it has made for itself.

Thurley, Geoffrey, "Tale of Two Cities." *The Dickens Myth: Its Genesis and Structure*. St. Lucia, Queensland: University of Queensland Press, 1976: 255–275.

A competent summary and analysis of the novel, with a focus on class structure and the duality represented by twinned characters like Charles Darnay and Sidney Carton, and opposing characters like Lucie Manette and Madame Defarge.

Contributors

Harold Bloom is Sterling Professor of the Humanities at Yale University. He is the author of 30 books, including *Shelley's Mythmaking* (1959), *The Visionary Company* (1961), *Blake's Apocalypse* (1963), *Yeats* (1970), *A Map of Misreading* (1975), *Kabbalah and Criticism* (1975), *Agon: Toward a Theory of Revisionism* (1982), *The American Religion* (1992), *The Western Canon* (1994), and *Omens of Millennium: The Gnosis of Angels, Dreams, and Resurrection* (1996). *The Anxiety of Influence* (1973) sets forth Professor Bloom's provocative theory of the literary relationships between the great writers and their predecessors. His most recent books include *Shakespeare: The Invention of the Human* (1998), a 1998 National Book Award finalist, *How to Read and Why* (2000), *Genius: A Mosaic of One Hundred Exemplary Creative Minds* (2002), *Hamlet: Poem Unlimited* (2003), *Where Shall Wisdom Be Found?* (2004), and *Jesus and Yahweh: The Names Divine* (2005). In 1999, Professor Bloom received the prestigious American Academy of Arts and Letters Gold Medal for Criticism. He has also received the International Prize of Catalonia, the Alfonso Reyes Prize of Mexico, and the Hans Christian Andersen Bicentennial Prize of Denmark.

Mei Chin is a fiction writer and food critic living in New York. Her work has appeared in *Fiction Magazine* and *Bomb Magazine*, and in 2005 she was awarded the James Beard Foundation's M.F.K Fisher Distinguished Writing Award.

Cates Baldridge chairs the Department of English at Middlebury College in Vermont. His published works include articles on *Wuthering Heights*, *Pendennis*, *Oliver Twist*, and *Agnes Grey*, and books on Graham Greene and dissent in the English Novel.

Sir James Fitzjames Stephen was an English jurist and journalist who was an important contributor to the *Pall Mall*

Gazette. He was also the author of *History of the Criminal Law of England* (1883).

Edwin M. Eigner is a professor of English at the University of California, Riverside.

John Gross is the author of *The Rise and Fall of the Man of Letters*. The former editor of the *Times Literary Supplement*, he is currently a literary and theatre critic for the *Sunday Telegraph*.

John B. Lamb teaches English at West Virginia University and is an editor at *Victorian Poetry*.

Carol Hanbery MacKay is a professor of English at the University of Texas, Austin. She has written on Dickens and Thackeray.

Leonard Manheim was the founder of *Literature and Psychology* and co-editor of *Hidden Patterns: Studies in Psychoanalytic Literary Criticism*. He was professor emeritus at the University of Hartford.

David Rosen is Assistant Professor of English at Trinity College in Connecticut. He is the author of *Power, Plain English, and the Rise of Modern Poetry*.

G.K. Chesterton was a prolific critic, poet, and a novelist who was known for both his studies of Chaucer and Charles Dickens, and also his mystery series *Father Brown*.

Sylvère Monod taught at the Sorbonne until 1982. He is the author of a variety of works on Charles Dickens, both in French and in English.

John Kucich is a Professor of English at the University of Michigan. He is the author of *Excess and Restraint in the Novels* *of Charles Dickens,* and *Victorian Afterlife: Postmodern Culture Rewrites the Twentieth Century.*

John Forster was an editor, literary agent, and attorney who was also a close friend of Charles Dickens. He was the author of Dickens's first definitive biography, *The Life of Charles Dickens.*

Andrew Saunders is a Professor in the Department of English Studies at Durham University. He has written and edited several volumes on Dickens, Anthony Trollope, and Victorian literature in general.

Acknowledgments

Baldridge, Cates. "Alternatives to Bourgeois Individualism in *A Tale of Two Cities.*" In *Studies in English Literature, 1500–1900* 30, no. 4, pp. 646–649. © 1990 by the Johns Hopkins University Press. Reprinted by permission.

Stephen, Sir James Fitzjames. "*A Tale of Two Cities.*" In *The Dickens Critics*, ed. George H. Ford and Lauriat Lane, Jr., pp. 43–45. © 1961 by Cornell University Press. Reprinted by permission.

Eigner, Edwin M. "Charles Darnay and Revolutionary Identity." In *Dickens Studies Annual* vol. 12, pp. 149–151. © 1983 AMS Press, Inc. Reprinted by permission.

Gross, John. "*A Tale of Two Cities.*" In *Dickens and the Twentieth Century*, ed. John Gross and Gabriel Pearson, pp. 189–192. © 1962 by the University of Toronto Press. Reprinted by permission.

Lamb, John B. "Domesticating History: Revolution and Moral Management in *A Tale of Two Cities.*" In *Dickens Studies Annual* vol. 25, pp. 238–241. © 1996 AMS Press, Inc. Reprinted by permission.

MacKay, Carol Hanbery. "The Rhetoric of Soliloquy in *The French Revolution* and *A Tale of Two Cities.*" In *Dickens Studies Annual* vol. 12, pp. 198–200. © 1983 AMS Press, Inc. Reprinted by permission.

Manheim, Leonard. "A Tale of Two Characters: A Study in Multiple Projection." In *Dickens Studies Annual* vol. 1, pp. 234–235. © 1970 AMS Press, Inc. Reprinted by permission.

Rosen, David. "*A Tale of Two Cities*: Theology of Revolution." In *Dickens Studies Annual* vol. 27, pp. 171–175. © 1997 AMS Press, Inc. Reprinted by permission.

Chesterton, G.K. "*A Tale of Two Cities*." In *Appreciations and Criticisms of the Works of Charles Dickens*, pp. 190–192. © 1970 Haskell House Publishers, Ltd. Reprinted by permission.

Monod, Sylvère. "Dickens's Attitudes in *A Tale of Two Cities*." In *Dickens Centennial Essays*, ed. Ada Nisbet and Blake Nevius, pp. 169–170. Originally published in *Nineteenth-Century Fiction*, Vol. 24, No. 4, The Charles Dickens Centennial (Mar., 1970). © 1970 by the University of California Press. Reprinted by permission.

Kucich, John. "The Purity of Violence: *A Tale of Two Cities*." In *A Tale of Two Cities*, ed. Harold Bloom, pp. 64–67. Originally published in *Dickens Studies Annual* vol. 8, pp. 238–241. © 1980 AMS Press, Inc. Reprinted by permission.

Forster, John. "The Tale of Two Cities." In *The Life of Charles Dickens*, pp. 730–732. © by 1928 Cecil Palmer. Reprinted by permission.

Saunders, Andrew. "Telling of Two Cities." In *Dickens and the Spirit of the Age*, pp. 102–105. © 1999 by Oxford University Press. Reprinted by permission.

Index

131